THINKING ABOUT
CHRISTIAN
APOLOGETICS

WHAT IT IS AND WHY WE DO IT

JAMES BEILBY

IVP Academic

An imprint of InterVarsity Press
Downers Grove, Illinois

InterVarsity Press
P.O. Box 1400, Downers Grove, IL 60515-1426
World Wide Web: www.ivpress.com
E-mail: email@ivpress.com

InterVarsity Press® is the book-publishing division of InterVarsity Christian Fellowship/USA®, a movement of students and faculty active on campus at hundreds of universities, colleges and schools of nursing in the United States of America, and a member movement of the International Fellowship of Evangelical Students. For information about local and regional activities, write Public Relations Dept., InterVarsity Christian Fellowship/USA, 6400 Schroeder Rd., P.O. Box 7895, Madison, WI 53707-7895, or visit the IVCF website at <www.intervarsity.org>.

All Scripture quotations, unless otherwise indicated, are taken from the Holy Bible, New International Version®. NIV®. Copyright ©1973, 1978, 1984 by International Bible Society. Used by permission of Zondervan Publishing House. All rights reserved.

Cover design: Cindy Kiple
Interior design: Beth Hagenberg
Images: Vincent McIndoe/Getty Images

ISBN 978-0-8308-3945-2

Printed in the United States of America ∞

Library of Congress Cataloging-in-Publication Data

Beilby, James K.
   Thinking about Christian apologetics: what it is and why we do it/
James K. Beilby.
      p. cm.
   Includes bibliographical references (p.   ) and index.
   ISBN 978-0-8303-3945-2 (pbk.: alk. paper)
   1. Apologetics   I. Title.
   BT1103.B45 2011
   239—dc23

2011023120

P	18	17	16	15	14	13	12	11	10	9	8	7	6	5	4
Y	25	24	23	22	21	20	19	18	17	16					

To my maternal grandfather
Albert Bender
who modeled for me a love of learning theology

CONTENTS

Preface. 9

1. What Is Christian Apologetics?. 11

2. Patristic and Medieval Apologetics. 37

3. Modern and Contemporary Apologetics 61

4. Varieties of Apologetics. 87

5. Philosophical Objections to Apologetics 113

6. Biblical and Theological Objections to Apologetics . . . 133

7. Doing Apologetics Well. 157

A Bibliography of Works on Christian Apologetics 185

Notes 201

Name and Subject Index 209

PREFACE

This is not a typical apologetics book. Those who are looking for responses to objections to Christianity or arguments for Christianity should look elsewhere. In this, the bibliography provided at the end of this book will be of some help. Rather, this is a book about apologetics. In this book I discuss the nature and goals of apologetics, different approaches to apologetics, objections to the idea or practice of apologetics, and how apologetics should be done. Too often, Christian apologists have either bypassed these important issues or given them cursory treatment. The assumption has been and continues to be that these issues do not need to be considered in depth because the answers are obvious.

The answers to these questions are not obvious. And answering them well is crucially important. When Christian apologists bypass these questions and immediately jump into the *important* work of giving answers and making arguments, all too often the result is negative. I don't mean to suggest that their arguments are automatically bad because they haven't reflected on the nature of apologetics. Rather, their approach often suffers when they fail to carefully consider (among other things) what the goals of Christian apologetics should be. I believe that the apologetic arguments for Christian belief can be powerful. But if they are not aimed with care and handled with an appropriate attitude, they can be dangerous. Done well, apologetics can draw people closer to the kingdom of God. Done poorly, apologetics can reinforce negative stereotypes and drive people away.

Every effort has been taken to make this book usable as a textbook for an introductory apologetics course. Key terms are typically italicized, and a list of important concepts is provided at the end of each chapter. The annotated bibliography at the end of the book will steer students toward some of the best books (some more popular, some more academic) that cover specific apologetic issues. Finally, while my approach to apologetics is unique in certain respects, every effort has been taken to make this discussion of apologetics useful to a wide variety of Christians.

No project such as this book comes about without substantial assistance. I must acknowledge all of my students, particularly those who, through their questions, have taught me much about the practice and theory of apologetics; the Alumni Council of Bethel University, who supported my research for this book; the International Center for Philosophy of Religion (and especially Mike Rea and Tom Flint), who gave me visiting scholar status and a place to hole up and write; and Faith Covenant Church in St. Petersburg, Florida, who graciously provided my family and me with lodging for four weeks while I was on sabbatical. I am also deeply indebted to former and current teaching assistants Jared Bangs, Laine Gebhardt, Brendan Lorentz, Shelli Poe, Heather Rollefson and Levi Tijerina, who assisted me with tracking down books and articles. And special mention must be made of several colleagues who read and commented on various drafts of the book: David Clark, Paul Eddy, William Norton and Alan Padgett. Finally, I want to thank my family. My father and mother have always sacrificially supported my academic work. And my wife, Michelle, and my kids, Sierra, Madeline, Zachary and Malia, have supported me in ways too numerous to mention. Their love provides me with a daily and tangible reminder of the love of God.

I

WHAT IS CHRISTIAN APOLOGETICS?

I. A BASIC DEFINITION

Apologetics is, in the simplest possible terms, the attempt to defend a particular belief or system of beliefs against objections. Contrary to popular misunderstanding, apologetics has nothing to do with apologizing or saying I'm sorry. The term derives from the Greek word *apologia* (a-pol-o-GEE-a) and was originally used in a legal context. An *apologia* was a defendant's reply to the accusations of the prosecution. In the context of ancient Greece, a plaintiff could respond to an accusation or *kategoria* with a defense or *apologia*. This defense involved the attempt to (literally) "speak away" the accusation (*apo*—"away," *logia*—"speech") to show that the accusation was false.

Socrates' defense before the Athenian court is the classic example of an apology. The accusation against him was that he corrupted the young, refused to worship the gods and created new deities. Plato's *Apology* is the surviving account of Socrates' attempt to demonstrate his innocence. But the term *apolo-*

> *Apologetics is, in the simplest possible terms, the attempt to defend a particular belief or system of beliefs against objections.*

getics might be applied to a wide variety of contexts. In opposition to those who would claim that Jack Nicklaus or Ben Hogan is most deserving of the designation best golfer of all time, I might deliver an apology for the idea that Tiger Woods deserves that honor. Or I might engage in political apologetics, arguing that the platform of a particular political party is to be preferred. Even in religious contexts, there are Hindu apologetics and Muslim apologetics. The type of apologetics at issue in this book, however, is Christian apologetics.

The word *apologetics* (in both the noun and verbal form) appears nineteen times in the New Testament. The word is used either to denote an answer that is given to a charge, objection or accusation leveled against an individual or a vindication (implying a successful answer or defense).

Consider the eight occurrences of the noun form of *apologia*. (The word for *apologia* has been italicized in each.)

Acts 22:1—"Listen now to my *defense.*" (Paul speaking to a Jewish mob in Jerusalem)

Acts 25:16—"It is not the Roman custom to hand over any man before he has faced his accusers and has had an opportunity to *defend* himself against their charges."

1 Corinthians 9:3—"This is my *defense* to those who sit in judgment on me."

2 Corinthians 7:11—"See what this godly sorrow has produced in you: what earnestness, what eagerness to *clear yourselves.*"

Philippians 1:7—"For whether I am in chains or *defending* and confirming the gospel, all of you share in God's grace with me."

Philippians 1:16—"Do so in love, knowing that I am put here

for the *defense* of the gospel."

2 Timothy 4:16—"At my first *defense,* no one came to my support."

1 Peter 3:15—"Always be prepared to *give an answer* to everyone who asks you to give the reason for the hope that you have."

In four of these passages, it is Paul himself that is being defended (Acts 22:1; Acts 25:16; 1 Cor 9:3; 2 Tim 4:16); in one passage it is the recipient of Paul's letter that has given a defense and been vindicated (2 Cor 7:11); and in three cases it is the gospel of Jesus Christ that is being defended (Phil 1:7, 16; 1 Pet 3:15). The last verse, 1 Peter 3:15, is probably the best-known verse on apologetics because it contains not only a clear reference to apologetics but a command to engage in it.

Of course, while the idea of presenting a rational defense of the gospel of Jesus Christ is clearly present in Philippians 1:7, 16 and 1 Peter 3:15 and is implied in many other texts, that does not mean that the Bible teaches about apologetics. There is no formal system or theory of apologetics found in the Bible. The Bible records instances of apologetics and commends the task to Christians, but it does not provide specifics on how apologetics should be done. In fact, it wasn't until the second century that the word *apologia* began to be applied not just to a task but to Christians engaged in that task.[1]

Nevertheless, from the biblical materials, the basic contours of Christian apologetics can be discerned. Christian apologetics involves an action (defending), a focus of the action (the Christian faith itself), a goal (upholding Christianity as true) and a context (the circumstances in which apologetics occurs). Consequently, in this chapter each of these elements will be discussed, as will the relationship between apologetics and related disciplines, such as evangelism and theology.

2. MAKING A DEFENSE

Because *apologia* is often translated as "defense," some have misunderstood the task of Christian apologetics to involve only responses to objections to the Christian faith. There are, however,
a good number of biblical passages that do not explicitly use the
term *apologia* that provide a more well-rounded picture of the
apologetic task. Four of the most commonly mentioned are as
follows:

> 2 Corinthians 10:5—"We demolish arguments and every
> pretension that sets itself up against the knowledge of God,
> and we take captive every thought to make it obedient to
> Christ."

> 2 Timothy 2:25—"Those who oppose [the servant of the
> Lord] he must gently instruct, in the hope that God will
> grant them repentance leading them to a knowledge of the
> truth."

> Titus 1:9—"[One who would be an elder] must hold firmly
> to the trustworthy message as it has been taught, so that he
> can encourage others by sound doctrine and refute those
> who oppose it."

> Jude 3—"I felt I had to write and urge you to contend for the
> faith that was once for all entrusted to the saints" (because
> some have been spreading false teachings about the gospel).

As these passages indicate, apologetics can involve a variety of
activities, including but not limited to "demolishing arguments,"
"contending for the faith," "refuting those who oppose sound doctrine" and "gentle instruction." Consequently, a more well-rounded
picture of apologetics is given by the phrase "defending and commending the faith." In other words, the action of apologetics includes two different (but complementary) aspects—one defensive
and the other offensive. An example of the defensive aspect of

apologetics is the attempt to respond to the claim that the existence of evil in the world entails that God cannot exist, or if he does exist that he cannot be all good or all-powerful, as Christians have traditionally claimed. Let's call this aspect of apologetics *responsive apologetics*. (Others have called this aspect of apologetics *negative* or *defensive* apologetics.) The goal of responsive apologetics is to demonstrate that objections to Christian belief are not successful.

In addition to responsive apologetics, a Christian might defend his or her religious belief by engaging in what I will call *proactive apologetics*. (Others have called this aspect of apologetics *positive* or *offensive* apologetics.) As the name implies, when engaging in proactive apologetics the Christian does not wait until a skeptic has developed an argument against Christianity. Rather, the Christian takes the initiative by giving arguments for Christian belief, arguments intended to show that Christian belief is perfectly rational or, perhaps, that Christian belief is intellectually superior to other worldviews. Those engaged in proactive apologetics would be likely to embrace the slogan "the best defense is a good offense." An example of proactive apologetics would be an argument for the existence of God, such as the teleological or design argument, or an argument for the reliability of the Bible.

But notice that it is possible to engage in proactive apologetics in two different ways. Arguments for the existence of God or the truthfulness of an aspect of Christian belief are *constructive apologetic arguments*. They seek to support or establish the truthfulness of the Christian worldview. But it is possible to engage in proactive apologetics in another way—by offering arguments against other worldviews and in so doing show that alternatives to the Christian worldview are deficient in one way or another. This would be a *deconstructive apologetic argument*. The goal of such an argument is refutation. Of course, deconstructive apologetic arguments do not establish the truthfulness of the Christian worldview. Even if a competitor to Christianity, say atheism, is false, that doesn't mean that Christianity is true. After all, it is logically possible that both are false. In fact, even if one demonstrated via deconstructive apologetic arguments that all the known competitors to Christianity were false, that wouldn't mean that Christianity was true. This is because it is logically possible (even if unlikely) that a worldview that no one has yet thought of is true. Nevertheless, deconstructive apologetic arguments are valuable. After all, when making decisions about which worldview is true, if a person is aware of arguments that suggest that the competitors to Christianity were probably false, that makes it easier to embrace Christian belief. Further, arguments against atheism might be sufficient to cause atheists to take more seriously arguments for Christian belief, arguments that had been previously dismissed.

Just as there are a couple of different ways of doing proactive apologetics, one might engage in responsive apologetics in two quite different ways. Take, for example, the argument against the possibility of miracles. One might respond to this argument by providing positive evidence for miracle claims. Such an approach, in effect, says to the objector, "You claim that miracles are not possible, but you must be wrong because I have good evidence for a particular event being miraculous." Call this a *rebutting apologetic argument*. But one might respond to the objection to miracles in a very different way, by arguing that the objection itself is problematic. Call this an *undercutting apologetic argument*.[2] Such an argument might involve the response that the objection to the possibility of the miraculous commits a logical fallacy or entails a philosophical stance that is problematic in important respects.

The essential difference, therefore, between rebutting and undercutting arguments is that rebutting arguments meet force with force: evidence against a proposition is countered with evidence for that proposition. In other words, objection O to Christian belief B is answered by providing reasons to believe B. Undercutting arguments, however, do not seek to offer an opposing side. Rather they seek to undercut the evidence being offered for a proposition by showing that the evidence being offered is flawed in one respect or another. In other words, objection *O* to Christian belief *B* is answered by providing reasons to reject *O*.

In summary, there are two different kinds of apologetic arguments, each of which has a pair of variations:

1. *Proactive apologetics:* demonstrating that belief in Christianity makes sense

   a. *Constructive arguments:* arguments for the truthfulness of Christianity

   b. *Deconstructive arguments:* arguments against the truthfulness of other worldviews

2. *Responsive apologetics:* demonstrating that objections to Christianity are unsuccessful

   a. *Rebutting arguments:* responses to an objection designed to support that which is being attacked

   b. *Undercutting arguments:* responses to an objection designed to show that the objection itself is misguided

Typical apologetic encounters will involve a complex of the various types of proactive and responsive apologetics. Which kind of apologetic argument is utilized depends on the situation, one's knowledge base and the apologetic topic being discussed.

3. DEFENDING THE CHRISTIAN FAITH

So apologetics is about defending and commending. But Christian apologetics is a particular variety of apologetics, one that defends and commends Christian belief. What is meant by the term *Christian*? And what about the term *Christian* does apologetics defend? Before seeking to answer this question, it is important to acknowledge that there are at least three different usages of the term *Christian*. First, *Christian* may be simply used as a cultural label or identifier. On this usage, a people are Christian if they call themselves Christian. Second, *Christian* can be used of those who have (or will have) the gift of salvation. Finally, *Christian* is used as a description of the beliefs Christians have embraced throughout history, the fundamental beliefs shared by Augustine, Aquinas, Calvin and Wesley. The first of these usages is generally uninteresting and dangerous if used to define what makes apologetics Christian (for some of what has been done by those who call themselves Christians cannot be defended). The second sense of *Christian* is also inadequate for understanding the sense in which Christian apologetics is Christian. Whether a person is saved is simply beyond our ken. We simply do not have access to the current disposition of a person's heart toward God, much less the future disposition of a person's heart. Consequently, the final usage of *Christian* is the appropriate one here. Christian apologetics seeks to defend what orthodox Christians have claimed about God throughout history.

> Christian apologetics
> seeks to defend what
> orthodox Christians have
> claimed about God
> throughout history.

But this does not mean that it is the task of Christian apologetics to defend everything that Christians believe. This is an all-too-common misunderstanding. On this mistaken view whether or not one accepts social trinitarianism or the substantial view of the *imago Dei* or an episcopal understanding of church government is an apologetic issue. But none of those issues is apologetic in nature. They are theological questions. Of course, this isn't to say that they are unimportant. Theological questions are very important, in many ways and for many reasons. Simply put, apologetics does not focus on questions that might be considered intramural debates between Christians, however theologically important those debates might be. Apologetics deals with core Christian issues, the essentials of the faith. In other words, what apologetics defends are the notions that if removed from a system of beliefs would eliminate the sense in which that system could be called Christian.

What are these core Christian beliefs? There is, of course, no simple answer to this question. There are undoubtedly theological beliefs on some Christian's essential list that are not on others. Nevertheless, there is a common core of beliefs that are expressed in the ecumenical councils (Nicaea, Constantinople, Ephesus and Chalcedon), affirmed by the ecumenical Christian creeds (the Apostles' Creed, the Nicene Creed and the Athanasian Creed), sustained by the major denominational divisions of the Christian church (Catholic, Protestant and Orthodox), and central to the basic teachings of the great theologians of the faith. Items on this list include the existence of God, the deity of Jesus Christ, the affirmation of God as Trinity, the claim that God created all that exists outside himself, the assertion of human sinfulness, the atonement of Jesus Christ and undoubtedly more. This is not to suggest that there are no disagreements on how to understand these core ideas. For example, there are numerous ways of explaining the atonement. To explain the unity and diversity of Christian belief, we need a distinction between dogmas and doctrines. Dogmas are the core Christian claims; doctrines are attempts to explain, apply and flesh out dogmas. The idea that our salvation was made possible by Jesus is a dogma; different explanations of how Jesus made our salvation possible are doctrines. Consequently, one who accepts the penal substitutionary theory of the atonement has doctrinal disagreements with one who accepts the Christus Victor theory, but they both accept the underlying dogma.

Here is the key idea: **The proper domain of apologetics is the defense of dogmas, not doctrines.** Again, this is not to say that doctrinal disputes are unimportant, only that they are theological in nature, not apologetic. And I fully acknowledge that this definition will result in the definition of some topics as apologetic where others define them as theological. But the potential muddiness of the dogma/doctrine distinction does not diminish its importance. Some such distinction is necessary to provide some understanding of the term Christian apologetics. What is being defended is Christianity, not some slice of Christianity such as Baptist apologetics or Calvinist apologetics.

Boiled down to its essentials, therefore, those who engage in Christian apologetics are defending and commending the gospel of Jesus Christ and whatever theological concepts are necessary to the gospel even while acknowledging that it is possible that some Christians will disagree as to what the gospel of Jesus Christ is and what theological concepts are essential to it.

4. THE GOALS AND LIMITATIONS OF APOLOGETICS

So apologetics is the defense of the essential beliefs of the Christian faith. But against what? Against the claim that the average member of other world religions is better looking than the average Christian? Against the claim that *Christianity* has more letters than *atheism* and that, therefore, atheism is the clearer, more straightforward worldview? Of course not. The first of these objections, even if true (and I'm in no position to deny it), is irrelevant, and the second is clearly fallacious. Simply put, the goal of apologetics is to defend and commend the truthfulness of Christian belief. This involves defending Christian belief against objec-

> *The goal of apologetics is to defend and commend the truthfulness of Christian belief.*

tions that seek to undercut or call into question the truthfulness of Christianity and offering substantial, thoughtful reasons to accept its truthfulness.

There are, however, few concepts more loaded or hotly debated in contemporary society than truth, so a couple words of explanation are in order. As I will use the term, truth is a property of statements or propositions. A statement or proposition is true if it is an accurate description of reality. Thus understood, truth is not simply a matter of coherence, intuitive appeal or pragmatic benefit. A coherent set of beliefs might be informative, but coherence is not the same thing as truth. J. R. R. Tolkien's *Lord of the Rings* is highly coherent, but that doesn't mean that you can visit Hobbiton or become a Facebook friend of Frodo Baggins. Similarly, the ideas of intuitive appeal and pragmatic benefit are notoriously unclear when applied to Christian beliefs. After all, according to certain standards apparently widely accepted in Western culture, any worldview that is not focused on the accumulation of wealth and pleasure is profoundly unappealing and monumentally impractical. Moreover, the relationship between both appeal and practicality and truth is tenuous at best. There are simply many beliefs that, while useful, are false. Adolf Hitler, for example, found the claim that the Jews were responsible for the economic woes in Germany in the mid and late 1920s very appealing and useful, even though it was false. And there are many beliefs that are true but are of little practical benefit to anybody, such as "the maple tree in our backyard was only four feet tall when I was ten years old." Of course, coherence, intuitive appeal or pragmatic benefit can be indicative of truth, but they are not the same thing as truth. In other words, the fact that a belief of yours is intuitively appealing and pragmatically useful might give you some reasons to believe that it is true, but it is not true just because it is intuitively appealing and pragmatically useful. (There is much more that can be said about the concept of truth; some of these matters are touched on in chapters five and seven.)

Given this understanding of the goal of apologetics—defending the truthfulness of Christian belief—how does one determine success? Here there are a variety of options. First, one might locate success in the argument itself. If you gave a good argument—an argument that should be compelling or convincing—then you have been successful. Some would press this idea further and claim that apologetic success occurs only when one has successfully proved the truth of Christian belief. Second, one might locate success not in the argument but in the response to the argument. Apologetics is successful when one's interlocutor is moved to some degree and in some way by what is said. Some take this idea further, arguing that apologetics should set as its goal nothing less than conversion, helping the person to whom you're talking commit his or her life to Jesus Christ. Anything less does not accomplish the ultimate goal.

Apologetic success, however, is neither strictly a matter of the quality of one's arguments nor the apparent response of your interlocutor. While the quality of one's arguments is certainly not irrelevant, this is also not the most important feature of apologetics. After all, it is possible to give profound and logically persuasive arguments but do so in a way that is arrogant, dismissive and thoroughly un-Christlike. Similarly, while in one sense apologetics should be focused on the response of one's interlocutor, it is possible to achieve a positive response through manipulation or shoddy arguments that will, upon closer inspection, fall to pieces. Consequently, apologetic success is best understood as faithfulness to Jesus Christ.[3] In our apologetic endeavors, we are called to be faithful to Christ in at least three senses. First, what we say should accurately represent who Jesus is, what he taught and, specifically, the good news he brought to the world. Second, the way we do our apologetics should augment our arguments, not detract from them. We must defend Christ in a way that fits with Christ's message. Finally, we must be faithful to God's purposes in specific situations. In some cases, apologetics appropriately and naturally leads to an offer for a person to commit her life to Christ, but in the vast majority of cases, our apologetic endeavors are a small step in a person's long and a winding journey that one hopes will culminate in relationship with Jesus Christ. Just as in 1 Corinthians 3:6 where the apostle Paul said, "I planted the seed, Apollos watered it, but God made it grow," our responsibility is to be faithful to our call in whatever

> *Apologetic success is best understood as faithfulness to Jesus Christ.*

situation God has placed us and help our interlocutor move one more step toward Christ, whether that step be merely acknowledging that not all Christians are morons or committing his life to Christ. In other words, we must approach each apologetic situation pneumatologically, acknowledging that the Holy Spirit has preceded us and will work after we have left. Our task is to discern what God requires of us in each situation.

Being faithful to Jesus Christ requires a broader picture of the task of giving sound reasons for the faith. Traditionally, the task of offering sound reasons to believe has been accomplished primarily by giving arguments for Christianity and against non-Christian perspectives. While arguments are important, they are only one of the ways apologetics encourage the development of Christian belief. More important than positive arguments for Christian belief is the task of clearing away impediments to belief. Sometimes these impediments are intellectual objections—such as the notion that science has disproved God's existence or that the existence of other religions makes it impossible to assert the truthfulness of Christianity. Other times, impediments to belief are based on misunderstandings of Christian teachings. Some think, for example, that the Trinity is the same as polytheism and

that all Christians homeschool their kids, believe that the King
James Version is the only inspired version of the Bible and believe
that AIDS is God's judgment on homosexuals. These are misunderstandings, and bringing some clarity to these issues can help
people take Christianity seriously. Even more important than the
task of clearing away impediments to belief, however, is the task
of being authentically Christian as you offer arguments, answer
objections and clarify issues. The attitude with which you engage
questions can itself either be a powerful apologetic for Christianity or a powerful deterrent. (More on this in chapter seven.)

In summary, therefore, the goal of apologetics is to offer sound
reasons to believe the Christian faith, reasons that (1) accurately
represent the gospel of Jesus Christ, (2) are presented in a Christlike manner, (3) address our interlocutor's questions and current
spiritual disposition, and (4) help the interlocutor move from a
position of basic mistrust (of God, Christianity, etc.) to a position
of basic trust—a position that will allow the person to eventually
commit his or her life to Jesus Christ.

Thus understood, Christian apologetics has some obvious limitations. These limitations should be acknowledged and embraced.
Christian apologetics does not and cannot do everything. And
there is no quicker, more certain path to undercutting the value of
apologetics than by trying to make it do everything.

First, apologetics cannot and should not provide what some
critics of Christianity desire—a revision of the fundamental ideas
and concepts of Christianity. Some who reject Christianity do so
because, like the noted twentieth-century New Testament scholar
Rudolf Bultmann, they believe that "it is impossible to use electric
light and the wireless and to avail ourselves of modern medical
and surgical discoveries, and at the same time to believe in the
New Testament world of spirits and miracles."[4] (A twenty-first-
century Bultmann would probably replace electric lights and the
wireless with solar technology and cell phones.) Others reject

Christianity because they profoundly dislike the idea of a God who defines morality and has moral expectations of them. In terms of getting these people to accept Christianity, it would be apologetically advantageous to reject the possibility of miracles or to allow each person to define morality for themselves. However, this is not an option. It must be acknowledged that some of the ideas of Christianity are profoundly countercultural, especially to many in the Western world in the twenty-first century. But to the degree apologetics seeks to water down that which the devout secularist deems to be unreasonable in Christian belief, it will cease to be Christian apologetics.

Second, apologetics cannot compel belief in Jesus Christ. Even if one's arguments and presentation are flawless, one's conversation partner might be completely unmoved. And that is because neither belief nor unbelief is brought about solely by intellectual arguments. Some reject Christianity because they were raised to be very suspicious of "judgmental holy-rollers"; others reject Christianity because they have been mistreated in one way or another by a person professing to be a devout Christian. The reasons for unbelief are incredibly diverse, and many of these reasons are hidden deep under psychological and personal baggage. Apologists must be sensitive to such issues, and they must realize that arguments alone will typically be powerless to overcome such deep-rooted anger and resentment. The road to healing for such people may include a healthy dose of apologetics, but it will likely be a long road and the majority of the freight will be carried by relationship and the inward working of the Holy Spirit.

> *The reasons for unbelief are incredibly diverse, and many of these reasons are hidden deep under psychological and personal baggage.*

Third, even if apologetics can help bring people to the place where they accept the truth of the essential teachings of Christianity, it cannot create faith. Through apologetic argument, a person might come to believe that God exists, that Jesus Christ is the Son of God and that salvation comes through committed relationship with Jesus. That person might even believe on the basis of solid apologetic arguments that he or she should commit to Jesus and that this decision is the most important one anyone could make. But this is not faith. Faith occurs when a person actually commits to Christ. To use an old adage, apologetics can bring the horse to water, but it cannot make it drink.

5. THE APOLOGETIC AUDIENCE AND CONTEXT

The final aspect of our definition of apologetics concerns the context in which apologetics occurs. There is an important distinction between audience and context. *Audience* is the person or persons to whom you are speaking; *context* is the environment in which your apologetic conversation occurs. There are as many different potential audiences for apologetics as there are people with questions about Christianity, but it is possible to categorize the apologetic audience in a couple of ways. First, there are a differences among private, public and academic apologetics. *Private apologetics* occurs in the context of conversations between individuals or small groups of people—around the water cooler at work, perhaps, or in a chance encounter with an acquaintance at a coffee shop. *Public apologetics,* on the other hand, is directed not at an individual or small group of individuals but at a general audience. Public debates, lectures and sermons are all public apologetics. So are many apologetic books. Even if they are written with a particular person in mind, they are disseminated to a general audience. Finally, there is *academic apologetics.* This form of apologetics is almost always written rather than verbal, and, by its nature, it operates at a very high level of complexity. Typically, the audience for academic apologetics is not specific. Consequently, the focus of academic apologetics is typically not on how the arguments will be heard but on whether the arguments are sound. This feature of academic apologetics has caused some to question its usefulness or even its appropriateness. However, if it is recognized that the arguments produced by academic apologetics must always be contextualized to a particular audience and situation, academic apologetics can be very helpful—even necessary. Academic apologetics helps refine apologetic arguments in the fire of academic debate, and academic debate is very helpful at exposing the potential weaknesses of arguments. Christian apologetics (either public or private, around the water cooler or from the pulpit) is much better off if the arguments being used have received thorough scrutiny.

But one might also categorize the audience of apologetics by the beliefs and attitudes of its recipients. The hearers of apologetics can be believers, agnostics or skeptics—that is, they might already accept the broad outline of Christian belief, they might not be sure what to think about Christian belief, or they might explicitly reject Christian belief. It might be surprising that believers are listed as a potential audience of apologetics, for it is commonly assumed that apologetics typically takes place only with agnostics or skeptics. Such an assumption tends to downplay the significance of the questions Christians have about the faith. Left unanswered, these can become toxic to continued vital faith. Moreover, in reality, apologetic conversations with skeptics and agnostics compose a relatively small percentage of the total number of actual apologetic conversations. It is far more common to have apologetic conversations with other Christians. This type of apologetics is called *internal apologetics* because it takes place with those inside of or internal to Christianity. Engaging in an apologetic conversation with skeptics or agnostics, those outside of or external to Christianity, is called *external*

apologetics. Of course, the distinction between internal and external should not be taken as expressing a soteriological divide
(who is saved and who is not). It is a matter of self-identification.
People are internal to Christianity if they call themselves Christian, if they self-identify with the Christian community and
worldview, and external if they do not. Where the goal of external apologetics is to encourage a change of mind in the skeptic,
the goal of *internal apologetics* is to reinforce faith, to remove
intellectual barriers, to help clarify issues and in so doing dispel
doubts. Internal apologetics is not only more common than external apologetics; it is usually more fruitful. Take, for instance,
a Christian who has lost a loved one and is struggling with the
problem of evil—if God is good and in control of his creation,
why does apparently meaningless suffering occur? This is a real
and profound question. More-
over, it is very likely not simply
an intellectual question. It is an
issue that is at once intellectual
and affective; it concerns the
heart as well as the mind. But
helping a Christian come to
some level of understanding on
this difficult matter is far easier
than doing the same with a
skeptic. The Christian most
likely already accepts certain ideas that make your work much
easier, such as the authority of Scripture or the possibility of
eternal life. Even more important, Christians typically want to
have their questions answered. They are usually well-motivated
and are likely to become more so as they sense progress toward
understanding.

Internal apologetics is less commonly practiced than it should
be. Perhaps this is because it is incorrectly assumed that the sole

> The goal of internal
> apologetics is to reinforce
> faith, to remove intellectual
> barriers, to help clarify
> issues and in so doing
> dispel doubts.

goal of apologetics is to convert non-Christians, perhaps it is because of lingering anti-intellectualism in Christianity, and perhaps it is because of fear of not knowing how to explain religious beliefs that one holds dear. If we just don't talk about topics like doubt and if we suppress honest, searching questions regarding the faith (both ours and those of others around us), then we won't have to admit to not having the answers to those questions. Regardless of the reason, apologetics should be an important part of every program of Christian education, whether in the home, in church or in an academic institution.[5]

There is a final apologetic audience. And it is probably the most common. Apologetics can (and often does) take place within a believer's own mind.[6] This would, of course, be a variety of internal apologetics! Unless one is actively avoiding thinking about the faith, one cannot be a Christian living in the contemporary world and be free from questions (and perhaps even authentic doubts) about various aspects of the faith. Why is there so much suffering in the world? Why does God not provide more obvious evidence of his existence? What is the salvific status of those who have never heard the gospel? Of course, these questions are not only apologetic in nature. Thoughtful Christians will have to engage a complex mixture of theological, spiritual, personal and psychological factors in answering these questions. But there is an unavoidably apologetic component to answering these questions. Therefore, when Christians obey the call to "take captive every thought" (2 Cor 10:5; compare Rom 12:1-2), this will necessarily involve shouldering the apologetic task of understanding and articulating the truth of Christian beliefs in the face of the sorts of questions that arise in today's world.

Just as there are many different apologetic audiences, there are probably an infinite number of apologetic contexts. And apologetics, if it is to be effective, must take into account the context. The specific apologetic context includes social, cultural and relational features. Apologetics that occurs within a small-group context is different from one-on-one apologetics, and apologetic conversations between close friends or family members are very different from conversations between complete strangers. Each of these unique situations has some advantages and some disadvantages. A small-group context can be less threatening than a one-on-one conversation, but conversations in small groups bring their own set of challenges, not the least of which is a difficulty of focusing on a single set of questions. Similarly, an apologetic conversation with a complete stranger is in some ways more difficult and some ways easier than an apologetic conversation with somebody you know very well. You do not know their history, personal idiosyncracies and particular sensitivities. And that makes understanding and being understood more difficult. On the other hand, imagine an apologetic conversation with an older sibling, a parent or your spouse. While you know their history and their issues, there is also a complex relational dynamic that makes apologetic conversations enormously difficult. One's parent (or even older sibling) might think: "Who is this kid to tell me about God? I taught him everything he knows!" And apologetic conversations with one's spouse are extremely difficult to keep separate from other typical issues between spouses: "Why are you always trying to change me?" Of course, engaging in apologetics with an awareness of context is difficult. But since it is obvious that contextual factors affect apologetic conversations, failing to take them into account is ludicrous. Apologetics needs to be context-sensitive and audience-specific.

> Christian apologetics is the task of defending and commending the truthfulness of the gospel of Jesus Christ in a Christlike, context-sensitive and audience-specific manner.

With this final clarification, we are in a position to offer a definition of Christian apologetics. Christian apologetics is the task of defending and commending the truthfulness of the gospel of Jesus Christ in a Christlike, context-sensitive and audience-specific manner.

6. APOLOGETICS AND RELATED DISCIPLINES

Our final topic in this introductory chapter is the relationship of Christian apologetics, as defined, to other disciplines. I will discuss four, in ascending order of importance: meta-apologetics, philosophy of religion, evangelism and theology.

Meta-apologetics. *Meta-apologetics* is a second-order discipline.[7] In other words, it is a discipline that analyzes another discipline. One engaged in meta-apologetics is interested in asking what apologetics is, how it should be done and what makes it effective. (I will discuss these and other meta-apologetic questions in chapter four.) The value of meta-apologetics should be obvious. It is difficult to do apologetics well if you don't understand the task itself or if you have not thought through the various questions embedded within the task. Consequently, even though meta-apologetics does not directly defend and commend the Christian faith, it supports apologists who do so. In fact, this book is not technically an apologetics book. It is an exercise in meta-apologetics.

Philosophy of religion. Philosophy of religion is also a second-order discipline. In this respect it is like meta-apologetics. But instead of analyzing apologetics, it analyzes the basic concepts and themes in religious traditions as well as the arguments for and against the claims made by adherents of those religious traditions. Consequently, Christian apologists have taken advantage of the arguments philosophers of religion have developed for God's existence and against atheistic interpretations of reality. Moreover, while it is possible (and even advantageous) to do philosophy of religion from the perspective of a particular religion (some call this religious philosophy or philosophical theology), philosophy of religion typically analyzes the concept of religion or a range of religious interpretations. Apologetics, on the other hand, is always pursued from the perspective of a particular religious tradition—Buddhist apologetics or Christian apologetics. Finally, philosophy of religion is focused just on the arguments that occur in inter-religious dialogue while apologetics focuses on both the arguments and how those arguments might be most effectively articulated. Apologetics, therefore, includes a practical dimension concerning the presentation of arguments not typically included in the philosophy of religion.

Evangelism. Evangelism and apologetics are closely related. Both have a common general goal: encouraging commitment to Jesus Christ. In fact, in certain theological circles, apologetics has been labeled pre-evangelism. On this understanding, apologetics clears the ground for evangelism; it makes evangelism more effective by preemptively addressing impediments to hearing the gospel. This is certainly true, but I submit that apologetics is also useful in the midst of the presentation of the gospel and after the presentation of the gospel. In other words, there is no moment in which a Christian takes off her evangelist hat and puts on her apologist hat. The relationship is more seamless than that. The difference between the two is one of focus. Evangelism is focused on presenting the gospel; apologetics focuses on defending and commending it. There is, moreover, an important difference in the audience of evangelism and apologetics. Evangelism is done only with non-Christians, but apologetics should be done with Christians and non-Christians alike.

Theology. The relationship between apologetics and theology is both crucially important and highly controversial. A few see apologetics and theology as being identical—to do apologetics is to do theology and vice versa. Others see the two as both conceptually and practically incompatible—doing theology makes apologetics unnecessary, and doing apologetics inevitably results in bad theology. Both of these perspectives are confused. Those who collapse theology and apologetics commonly misunderstand the nature and task of theology, and those who see apologetics as antithetical to theological commonly misunderstand the task and goal of apologetics.

But even among those who acknowledge the compatibility of apologetics and theology, there is a range of different ways of conceptualizing the relationship between the two. Some place *apologetics before theology,* asserting that one must establish fundamental theological facts (God's existence, that he has revealed himself, the reasonableness of trusting God's revelation, etc.) before theology can proceed. Thus B. B. Warfield defines the task of apologetics as "to investigate, explicate and establish the grounds on which a theology—a science, or systematized knowledge of God—is possible."[8]

Others reverse the order, placing *apologetics after theology,* holding that apologetics can only proceed after theological analysis has defined the concepts and beliefs that can be defended and commended to the world. John Calvin provides a clear example of this approach:

> Unless this certainty, higher and stronger than any human judgement, be present, it will be in vain to fortify the authority of Scripture by arguments, to establish it by common agreement of the church, or to confirm it with other helps. For unless this foundation is laid, its authority will always remain in doubt. Conversely once we have embraced it devoutly as its dignity deserves, and have recognized it to be above the common sort of things, those arguments—not strong enough before to engraft and fix the certainty of Scripture in our minds—become very useful aids.[9]

The mistake in each of these ways of relating apologetics and theology is the assumption that if there is a difference between the two—and there surely is—the difference must be chronological: we do one first and the other second. A better construal of the relationship between apologetics and theology is to see *apologetics with theology*. Apologetics comes as part of the theological enterprise because the Christian theologian claims that the theological core of the gospel is neither expendable nor negotiable—it is true and true in the sense of being an accurate description of reality. But, in the words of Kevin Vanhoozer, it is absolutely crucial that apologetics "should not proceed as if Christian doctrines were irrelevant to the defense, or to the understanding, of faith."[10] Only a theologically well-grounded, confident faith can engage in apologetics.

> *Only a theologically well-grounded, confident faith can engage in apologetics.*

Of course, this is not to conflate theology and apologetics. While they are not neatly separable, neither are they the same thing. Emil Brunner explains that theology is primarily oriented toward the thing proclaimed (God and his revelation) and apologetics is oriented toward the hearer of the proclamation.[11] This is helpful as long as it is acknowledged that theologians care about how their theology is heard and apologists care about being faithful to Jesus Christ. It must be understood that apologetics is neither a necessary precondition to theology nor an easily dispensable add-on. Apologetics is what happens when the Christian humbly yet confidently proclaims the good news of the gospel of Jesus Christ in a world where truth and reasons for belief matter.

KEY TERMS
proactive apologetics *demonstrating that Christian belief makes sense*
responsive apologetics *demonstrating objections are unsuccessful*

constructive apologetic arguments *for truthfulness*
deconstructive apologetic arguments *against truthfulness of world views*
rebutting apologetic arguments *support what is attacked*
undercutting apologetic arguments *shows objections to be misguided*
audience *those who listen*
context *the environment of the questions*
private apologetics *conversations between persons about Christianity*
public apologetics *directed at general audiences*
external apologetics *to those outside Christianity*
internal apologetics *between other Christians*
academic apologetics *written sound responses*
meta-apologetics *analysing other apologetics*
apologetics before theology *establishing fundamental theology first*
apologetics after theology *defending & commending theology after fact*
apologetics with theology *a part of theology*

2

PATRISTIC AND MEDIEVAL
APOLOGETICS

Before there was apologetics, there was a message. But almost immediately, the proclamation of the good news of Jesus Christ gave rise to questions and objections from Jews and Gentiles, from believers, inquirers and adversaries.[1] Many of the claims made by Christians stood in stark contrast to the intuitions, theological assumptions and philosophical arguments of the day. Consequently, Christians were called to support the preaching of the good news with a reasoned defense. In the next two chapters, I will discuss the impressive variety of ways Christians throughout the ages have sought to defend the truthfulness of Christian belief.

I. THE NEW TESTAMENT
While none of the books of the New Testament is an apologetic text in a systematic sense, most contain an awareness of apologetic issues and exhibit apologetic concerns.[2] New Testament writings seek to demonstrate the credibility of the essential claims of the gospel, particularly the life, teachings and resurrection of Jesus. Moreover, New Testament writers were intensely concerned

to protect the Christian teachings from perversions, both from within and from outside the church.

The Gospels. The Gospels do not look like works of apologetics. Their narrative form and lack of sustained argumentation seem to suggest that their goal is to tell a story rather than to defend it. Nevertheless, the Gospel writers were concerned not only to relate the message of Jesus but to do so in a way that was persuasive to their audience. The essential thrust of each of the four Gospels is to answer the question: Who is Jesus? And, as James Sire says, "The answer the Gospels give is itself an apologetic."[3] We see, know and trust God because we see, know and trust Jesus—God in flesh who was sent to reveal God to us. The best reason to commit yourself to God in faith is Jesus. In fact, it is very plausible to see one of the purposes of the Gospels as apologetic, to sustain the faith of early Christians in the face of attacks from Jews and Gentiles.

> *New Testament writings seek to demonstrate the credibility of the essential claims of the gospel.*

In this regard, a number of topics in the Gospels have a particularly clear apologetic focus. Most of them center on demonstrating that the life, death and resurrection of Jesus fulfilled a whole range of Old Testament prophecies. The first concerns the origins of Jesus. In the Jewish tradition it was clear that the Messiah must be in King David's royal line. Consequently, Gospel writers, particularly those writing to a Jewish audience, were concerned to demonstrate that Jesus was in David's line (as required by 2 Sam 7:12-13; Ps 89:3-4; 132:11-12; and Dan 9:25) and that he was born in Bethlehem (as required by Mic 5:2). The second concerns the widespread failure of the Jews to recognize Jesus as Messiah. All four Gospel writers (and Luke in Acts 28:26-27) answer this charge by citing Isaiah 6:10, which asserts that God himself blinded those who listened to Isaiah and prevented them from understanding. Avery Dulles goes so far as to claim that the usage of Isaiah 6:10 "was doubtless one of the pillars of primitive apologetic."[4]

First Peter 3:15. Perhaps the most famous New Testament passage on apologetics is 1 Peter 3:15. It's called the "apologetic mandate" because in it Peter instructs believers to "be prepared to give an answer to everyone who asks you to give the reason for the hope that you have." While the context of the passage is persecution of Christians, there is nothing in the text to suggest that "reasons for the hope within" should only be given in such settings. Moreover, the Greek word translated as "reason" is *logos* and suggests a logical, carefully considered explanation. Finally, not just any defense will do, for in 1 Peter 3:15, Peter clearly instructs his audience (likely, Christians in Asia Minor) to make a defense with the proper attitude—out of "gentleness and respect."

Acts 17:1-9. In the early verses of Acts 17, Paul presents an apologetic argument to those assembled in the synagogue in Thessalonica. Since he was in a Jewish synagogue, he assumed that his audience was familiar with the Hebrew Scripture and argued from it. His claim was that the Hebrew Bible taught not that the Messiah would inaugurate and rule Israel as Jewish people thought but that the Messiah would suffer, die and be resurrected. The result was mixed. While some Jews, quite a few "God-fearing" Greeks and women were persuaded, the majority were "were thrown into turmoil," forcing Paul and Silas to flee from the city fearing for their lives. Notice also that, while in 1 Peter 3:15 apologetics is a response to persecution, in Acts 17:1-9 it precedes persecution. This fact is supportive of what was claimed in the previous paragraph, that the apologetic mandate in 1 Peter 3:15 applies to all Christians, not just those being persecuted, for if apologetics was only a *response* to persecution, what is Paul doing in Acts 17:1-9?

Acts 17:16-34. After leaving Thessalonica, Paul eventually ended up in Athens. And while he continued his practice of speaking to the Jews at the local synagogue, he also delivered a speech at the Areopagus to the "men of Athens." Because this is an example of Paul speaking to an exclusively non-Jewish audience, many see it as a paradigm example of external apologetics, defense of the faith given to nonbelievers. (Another example is found in Acts 14:8-18.) And Paul's approach here is strikingly different from the one he used in Thessalonica. Since the Athenians did not know the Scriptures and wouldn't have accepted them as authoritative if they had, Paul did not appeal to biblical support but instead quoted a Stoic poet in support of his argument (Acts 17:24-29). In fact, Paul made no mention of Jesus or Christ, choosing instead to use a common Greek form of speech called a philosophical address. In his argument, Paul appealed to the Athenian's altar "to an unknown God" and declared that God has revealed himself and that the resurrection was proof of God's intention to judge the world. It is important to note that while Paul utilized concepts and argument forms familiar to his audience, he was unwilling to water down the gospel in any respect. In fact, he included a clear reference to the physical incarnation and resurrection of Jesus, despite the fact that most of those in his Greek audience would find such an idea ludicrous.

2. THE PATRISTIC ERA

As the church spread throughout the Roman Empire, it was confronted by a host of new challenges. Rabbinic Judaism, Gnosticism, paganism, and Greek and Roman philosophers all emphasized ideas in direct conflict with the gospel. During this period, three types of apologetic arguments were prevalent. First, *political apologetics* sought to win civil toleration of Christianity in the face of waves of persecution throughout the period from Nero (64) to Diocletian (284-305). The Romans had been willing to overlook Christianity as a sect of Judaism, but as it became clear that Christianity and rabbinic Judaism disagreed on very important matters, the Romans began to see Christianity as a threat to the stability of the eastern Mediterranean region. Many Jews undoubtedly did what they could to encourage this assumption. In this context, Christian apologists were forced to answer not only issues of theological substance ("Is Jesus really the Messiah?"), but also misunderstandings of Christian practices and beliefs: cannibalism ("This is my body, take and eat"), incest ("brothers and sisters" sharing a "holy kiss") and atheism ("You will have no other gods before me").[5] In fact, judging by the prevalence of responses of patristic apologists, the charge that Christians engaged in immoral behaviors must have been quite widespread.[6] Political apologetics sought to demonstrate the antiquity of Christian beliefs and sought to show that Christians were no threat to political stability.

In addition, to political apologetics, Christians in the early church also engaged in *religious apologetics,* or the attempt to demonstrate the superiority of Christianity over other religious or philosophical options, primarily Judaism and the various schools of Greek philosophy.

> Political apologetics sought to demonstrate the antiquity of Christian beliefs and sought to show that Christians were no threat to political stability.

Converts to Christianity were especially well motivated to engage in religious apologetics in order to explain the reasons for their conversion. Their apologetic arguments had both an external and an internal focus; they were designed both to win new converts and to furnish Christians with an armory of responses to adherents of other religious traditions. Christians engaging in religious apologetics had in their possession ample material with which to develop arguments against other religions. In particular, many patristic apologists were converts and therefore brought firsthand knowledge of their former belief systems. Against paganism,

Christian apologists often followed patterns of argument common in Hellenistic academic debates and took great advantage of the arguments of Greek philosophers (such as Zeno) against polytheism and idolatry. Christians' apologetic efforts against paganism also benefited from the efforts by Hellenistic Jews (such as Philo) to establish that Mosaic revelation was at least more ancient than that of the Gentiles and perhaps was the source for Greek philosophy.[7] Against the Jews, Christian apologists developed arguments designed to demonstrate that Old Testament prophecies had been fulfilled in Jesus Christ and that Jewish religious leaders had misused the Old Testament by becoming superstitious in their observation of the Law.[8] Curiously (to contemporary Christians), the miracles of Jesus did not play a prominent role in patristic apologetics. Christians in the first three centuries were concerned to distinguish their faith from pagan religions that attempted to claim legitimacy through the working of signs, wonders and miracles.[9]

A third species of apologetic argument very common in the patristic era addressed the beliefs of those who claimed the label Christian but held theological positions deemed to be in conflict with the teachings of Scripture. Some of these heretical views were examples of syncretism, the combining of Christian and non-Christian beliefs. For example, the Hellenistic disparagement of the material realm influenced a heresy called docetism (from the Greek *dokeō*, "to appear or seem"). Docetism included a denial of the full humanity of Jesus—he only appeared to have a human body. Another heresy in the patristic period was Gnosticism. Gnosticism was a complex arrangement of mythologies, the essence of which was that matter was evil and that enlightenment comes through spiritual awakening brought on by apprehension of hidden knowledge (*gnosis*). By the second century, Gnostic accounts of Jesus' teachings such as the *Gospel of Thomas* and the *Gospel of Truth* had to be refuted by Christians. But the best-known heresy in the early church was Arianism, which involved the claim that Jesus was not fully God, because God's essence could not be contained in a contingent, imperfect human being. Eusebius and Athanasius played significant roles in bringing Arian theology for consideration at the Council of Nicaea (325). While Nicaea explicitly condemned Arianism, Christian apologists had to contend with it well into the Middle Ages.

While there are many important patristic apologists, I will take a closer look at only three: Justin Martyr, Origen and Augustine.

Justin Martyr (100-165). Justin Martyr was the first well-known Christian apologist in the early church. His writings were diverse, addressing both religious and political apologetic issues, and his audience included Jews as well as Gentiles. Justin's *First Apology* (ca. 155) was addressed to the Roman emperor and argued that the charges brought against Christians were baseless and that Christians were no danger to the Roman Empire. In his *Second Apology* (ca. 161), Justin made his famous claim that "pagan philosophers, being enlightened by the divine *logos,* were in some sense Christians without knowing it."[10] And in *Dialogue with Trypho the Jew* (ca. 155-160), Justin revealed that his conversion from paganism to Christianity was the result of a study of Old Testament prophecy. He then engaged in religious apologetics by developing an argument for the divinity and messiahship of Jesus from Old Testament prophecies. He also responded to various Jewish objections to Christianity and claimed that the church was the new Israel.

Justin's apologetic efforts must be judged to be a mixed bag. While he effectively refuted some of the misunderstandings of Christianity common in Hellenistic society, his arguments for the antiquity of Scripture and for the Mosaic source of Greek philosophy and culture are not persuasive. Further, some of his arguments have unintended negative effects. For example, in his desire to utilize the philosophies of his day to demonstrate the truthfulness of Christianity, Justin Martyr clearly went too far. In his attempt to provide common ground between Christianity and pagan philosophy, he argued that all who follow the *logos* (reason) were in fact Christians. While such a claim elevated Christianity to the level of pagan philosophies, it undercut the ability of Christians to demonstrate the uniqueness of Christianity among pagan philosophies.

Origen (184-254). The most significant apologetic work from the first three centuries is Origen's *Contra Celsum* (ca. 248). While head of the catechetical school in Alexandria, *Origen* published a lengthy response to philosophical, historical and ethical criticisms of Christianity by the pagan Celsus, who held that Christianity was corrupting the traditions that held Hellenistic society together. His response is wide-ranging and detailed. In the course of Origen's reply, he considers the problem of evil, what is meant by Scripture, and the resurrection of the body. Central to his apologetic, however, is the historicity of Scripture and the deity of Jesus Christ. Origen defends the historicity of the Bible against objections, noting that Celsus's demands for historical proof cannot be met by any historical event, even those universally accepted. And Origen responds to Celsus's criticism of the person of Jesus with an argument for the divinity of Jesus that proceeds "first from Messianic prophecies, then from Jesus's miracles, and finally from the traces of miraculous power still to be found among the Christians, especially when the minds of those who accept the gospel are marvelously filled with peace and joy."[11]

Despite the fact that Origen himself held some heterodox theological views, his apologetic contribution is significant for a number of reasons. Some of Origen's arguments have become classics and are used, often without knowledge of their source, up to this day. For example, Origen offered an impressive (and commonly used) response to Celsus's claim that the disciples were hallucinating when they thought they saw the resurrected Jesus. More important for this study of the history of apologetics, however, is the fact that Origen's work represents a significant step forward in the development of Christian apologetics. He does not merely argue that Christianity should be politically or intellectually tolerated. Instead he launches a well-developed counteroffensive against a range of Jewish and pagan arguments against Christianity.

Augustine (354-430). The unquestioned apologetic giant of the patristic period is Aurelius *Augustine.* He occupies a unique place in the history of the Christian church because he is one of the few figures revered equally by Catholics and Protestants. Moreover, Augustine's apologetic works are unique in their systematic and holistic nature. Previous apologists were content to win their apologetic battles, but Augustine seeks to locate his approach to defending the faith in a thoroughly developed philosophical and theological framework.[12] Further, Augustine's significance is magnified by the fact that he stands at a pivotal juncture of the development of the church. As a transitional figure, with a foot in the early church and a foot in the Middle Ages, during Augustine's life the effects of Constantine's conversion to Christianity were fully realized. In fact, the burgeoning growth of Christianity provided a new apologetic argument for Christian apologists, who saw it as evidence of God's hand in history. It was left to preachers such as John Chrysostom to temper this enthusiasm with a recognition of the failure of Christians to live in accordance with the moral standards of the gospel.[13]

> *Augustine's apologetic works are unique in their systematic and holistic nature.*

While Augustine spent a great deal of time defending Christianity from heresies that arose from within the church, such as the Donatists and Pelagians, he also developed arguments against positions outside the church, including pagans, Jews and especially the Manicheans, a sect of which he was a member for a number of years. Against the Jews, he developed arguments drawing on the fulfillment of prophecy that were both more widely ranging than previous apologists and far more gracious in tone than many of his contemporaries and most of his apologetic progeny. And against the Manicheans, Augustine focused primarily on their response to the problem of evil, refuting their separation of good and evil into two eternal domains and offering instead a neoplatonic notion of evil as a privation or lack of good.

Augustine's apologetic magnum opus is undoubtedly *The City of God* (413-427), written to answer charges that the sack of Rome in 410 was due to the rejection of the pagan gods. As the most thorough refutation of pagan religions, it was "eminently successful and doubtless did much to undermine whatever prestige paganism still enjoyed at that time."[14] In the second half of *The City of God,* Augustine developed a theology of history from creation to the eschaton. Embedded in his theological reflections were apologetic arguments that pointed to the size, antiquity and relative unanimity of the church, the miracles of Christ, and fulfilled prophecy. Finally, in *The City of God* and in many of his other works, Augustine set his apologetic work in the context of a thorough analysis of the relationship between faith and reason. While he did not have the final word on this perennial problem, Augustine's articulation of the importance of reason and the reasonability of faith set the tone for apologetic work in the Middle Ages.

3. THE MIDDLE AGES

The advent of the Middle Ages inaugurated a period that has come to be known as Christendom—a period in which the Christian church dominated Western civilization, culture and even politics. By the eighth century, Christianity had co-opted pagan holidays and festivals and forced paganism underground. The increasing dominance of Christianity did not, however, contribute to the quality of religious apologetics, especially in the West. While the quality of apologetics in the East was maintained to some degree by constant contact with Zoroastrianism, Manichaeism and Islam, the Western church focused its efforts on civilizing the barbarians. Religious apologetics with Jews was also of generally poor quality during the Middle Ages. While medieval apologists adopted many of the arguments of Augustine, they generally did not emulate the graciousness of his style. Vehement diatribes and wholesale dismissal of Judaism were both justified with the contention that the church was the new Israel since the Jews had rejected Jesus. Islam was a different story. While it was initially dismissed by many Christians as a version of Arianism, the situation changed dramatically as Islam grew in power and represented a political and military as well as a religious and apologetic challenge. In fact, as Dulles notes, "the situation of Christendom vis-à-vis Islam was radically altered first by the failure of the Crusades to bring Islam to its knees and second by the penetration of Arab culture and science into the Western world."[15]

> *By the eighth century, Christianity had co-opted pagan holidays and festivals and forced paganism underground.*

In addition to these external apologetic challenges, apologists in the Middle Ages sought to address a matter of internal apologetic relevance—they sought to determine the rational grounds for the Christian faith.[16] These two goals were, in fact, related in important ways. Engaging in religious apologetics against Jews and Muslims required medieval apologists to offer rational reasons for matters of faith. Alan of Lille (d. 1202), for example, sought to rely solely on rational arguments for the truth of various Christian doctrines because he was convinced that Muslims could not be persuaded by arguments from Scripture.[17] The result of their work was not "the medieval view of the relationship between faith and reason" but a range of perspectives, the polarities of which symbolized a tension that has been with the Christian faith since its inception—"an apologetically inclined mentality, which seeks to find as broad a common ground as possible with the non-Christian, and a strictly dogmatic stance, which would safeguard the integrity of the faith even at the price of placing severe limits on the free exercise of reason."[18] While the extreme views were given ample expression by Peter Abelard (1079-1142), who had an unbridled emphasis on reason, and Bernard of Clairvaux (1090-1153), whose distrust of reason was profound, one of the best efforts at synthesis was that of Anselm.

Anselm (1033-1109). While *Anselm,* the archbishop of Canterbury, wrote on a number of important apologetic topics, most of his works address (at least tangentially) the relationship between faith and reason. Throughout his works, Anselm started with what he knew by faith, the content of Scripture and the teachings of the creeds, and sought to understand it by grasping the reasons that underlay the data of faith. In *Why God Became Man* (ca. 1098), Anselm crafted a dialogue between himself and the monk Boso in which he argued that the incarnation was necessary to achieve human salvation. While it was undoubtedly used as an apologetic argument against Jews, Anselm said that this book was not intended to help Christians "approach faith by way of reason, but in order to delight in the comprehension and contemplation of the doctrines they already believe."[19] "Right order," he said, "requires us to believe the deep things of the Christian faith before we undertake to discuss them by reason."[20] Further, Anselm held that while the theologian seeks reasons for his Christian beliefs, his faith in no way depends on the success of his arguments. Nevertheless, Anselm also held that "faith is a restless form of knowledge, always in search of the intrinsic reasons that account for its own data and make them able to be assimilated to a man's faculty of understanding."[21]

This restlessness was perhaps the motivation for Anselm to develop an argument that has fascinated, befuddled and annoyed Christians for centuries: the ontological argument. In his book, the *Monologion* (ca. 1078), he developed an argument the essence of which is that to properly understand the idea or concept of God is to understand that he must exist. Whether this argument works or not is hotly debated to this day; it is also debated whether Anselm intended this argument as a proof of God's existence. On the one hand, in the preface he stated that he believed that he had offered an argument that compelled the assent of the "fool" who denies God's existence. On the other hand, since in the *Monologion* the ontological argument was articulated as a prayer and was written to fellow monks who already embraced God's existence, many have speculated that Anselm's argument was intended to provide rational basis for what one already believed by faith.[22] That construal of the ontological argument would fit well with Anselm's other reflections on the nature of faith and reason.

It is interesting to note that even if Anselm saw his ontological argument as an exercise of understanding what is first accepted by faith, he clearly still had a very high view of human reason. In his refutation of the heresies of Roscelin of Compiégne, his argument proceeded solely by human reason because that was the means by which Roscelin defended himself and because scriptural arguments were useless since Roscelin either did not accept the authority of Scripture or read it so wrongly.

Peter the Venerable (1094-1156). As Abbot of Cluny, *Peter the Venerable* was one of the most influential religious apologists of the Middle Ages. The tone of his apologetic works was a vast improvement on many of his fellow medieval apologists. While many of the works against the Jewish faith were aimed at instructing Christians in how to respond to Jewish objections, Peter's (somewhat misleadingly titled) book *Against the Inveterate Obstinacy of* *the Jews* was designed to be read by Jewish people. Peter's heart for the conversion of the Jewish people led him not only to offer arguments from the Christian Scriptures but to respond to objections flowing out of the Hebrew text of the Bible and the Talmud. His argument for Christianity flowed from Jewish prophecy, which he argued foretold the coming of Jesus as Messiah, his atoning work and his establishment of the kingdom of God.

During Peter's lifetime, the First and Second Crusades affected the apologetic map of Western Europe greatly. Peter firmly believed that success would only be achieved if the military aspects of the Crusades were supplemented by apologetic and evangelistic efforts.[23] To that end, Peter commissioned a translation of the life of Muhammad and the Qur'an into Latin, wrote a short summary of Islamic doctrine, and wrote a refutation of Islam titled *A Book Against the Sect or Heresy of the Saracens*. His argument was that since the Qur'an acknowledged the authority of the Christian Scriptures and since the Christian Scriptures acknowledged only the divinity and authority of Jesus, Muslims who accepted the authority of the Qur'an ought to reject Muhammad and embrace Jesus.

Shortly after Peter the Venerable's death, apologetic dialogue between Christians and Muslims was taken to a new level by the Spanish Arab Averroes (1126-1198). Although deemed unorthodox by his fellow Muslims, Averroes developed and made popular a powerful synthesis of religious thought and Aristotelian philosophy. His commentary on Aristotle's work spread throughout Western Europe about the same time Aristotle's primary philosophical works were being recovered, edited and translated. His commentary became so well known that he himself became known in the Middle Ages as the Commentator. The effect of Averroes's introduction of Aristotle to Christendom is difficult to overstate. As Dulles notes, "For the first time since the Patristic Age, Christians were offered a scientific vision of the universe that did not depend on the religious imagery of the Bible."[24] The ensuing religious crisis was met first by Albert the Great (1193-1280) but more fully by his famous student, Thomas Aquinas.

Thomas Aquinas (1225-1274). *Thomas Aquinas* is the unquestioned titan of the medieval theological landscape, and his influence on Christian apologetics has been similarly profound. His *Summa Theologica* (written between 1265 and 1274) has provided theological material for apologetic encounters to this very day. And his *Summa Contra Gentiles,* subtitled *On the Truth of the Catholic Faith Against the Errors of the Unbelievers* (written between 1258 and 1264), was explicitly apologetic in intention. Aquinas's goal was to incorporate the insights of Aristotelian philosophy into Christianity and in so doing provide an authentically Christian alternative to Averroes and his Greco-Arabic worldview.

Following his teacher, Albert the Great, Thomas Aquinas made a distinction between beliefs that could be known through human reason and those that must come from divine revelation or be accepted on the authority of the church. In the first class he placed the belief that God exists, that he is one and that the pinnacle of human happiness can be found only in contemplating God; in the latter class he placed beliefs concerning the incarnation, Trinity, resurrection of the body and the end times. Of course, Aquinas acknowledged that some beliefs, such as the belief in God's existence, came from both reason and revelation. This is appropriate, said Thomas, for if knowledge of God came only by reason, only a few would attain such knowledge, and only after much study and with the potential of many errors. And while Aquinas did allow that arguments may be offered for beliefs that are beyond reason, he counseled that "this should be done for the training and consolation of the faithful, and not with the idea of refuting those who are adversaries. For the very inadequacy of the arguments would rather strengthen them in their error, since they would imagine that our acceptance of the truth of faith was based on such weak arguments."[25] But even if the Trinity or the incarnation cannot be proven by reason, it is possible, said Thomas, to refute heretical views of such doctrines. In fact, *Summa Contra Gentiles* included extended refutations of common heretical views. Moreover, while it was not an explicitly religious apologetic treatise, *Summa Contra Gentiles* included ample material for religious apologetics. Against the Jews, Thomas preferred arguments from miracles and the conversion of the world to the arguments from prophecy popular in the patristic age. And against Islam, Thomas contrasted the spread of Christianity with the spread of Islam. Muhammad, he said, acquired converts through promises of carnal pleasure where Christianity gained converts in the ancient world despite the fact that such worldly pleasures were restricted.

> Thomas Aquinas made a distinction between beliefs that could be known through human reason and those that must come from divine revelation or be accepted on the authority of the church.

Apologists of the early Middle Ages sought to correct the errors of the Greeks and Romans in light of Christian truth, but they accepted many of the philosophical forms and concepts of Platonism. It is a live question whether they conceded too much to their philosophical opponents.[26] Further, the universality of the Christian faith during the Middle Ages was not an unmitigated blessing to the exercise of Christian apologetics. The Christian faith "was taken for granted by most of the European populations. It was simply a part of the air they breathed."[27] The result of the universality of the Christian faith in the West was twofold. First, there was relatively little opportunity for meaningful interactions with those of other worldviews. Therefore, many of the descriptions of other worldviews by medieval apologists were caricatures. Too many of the apologetic encounters that did occur were unduly rhetorical and dismissive. Few Christian apologists approached their interlocutors with the attitude of Peter the Venerable, who approached Muslims not "as our people often do, by arms, but by words; not by force, but by reason; not in hatred, but in love."[28] Second, while patristic apologetics was given a boost by the success of the church, medieval apologetics benefitted from the setbacks of Christendom. The failure of the Crusades and the inroads of Arabic thought into Western Europe stimulated Christian apologetics in the Middle Ages because they forced Christians to engage ideas that were contrary to Christian belief in ways that they would not have had to if those setbacks had not occurred.

4. THE LATE MIDDLE AGES

Like Augustine and Anselm before him, Aquinas had tried to forge a synthesis between faith and reason. The reaction to Aquinas's synthesis was diverse. Some found in Aquinas too much of an emphasis on reason. For example, John Duns Scotus (1264-1308) sought to correct what he saw as an overemphasis on the intellect and a disparagement of the role of the will. Following his Greek philosophical heritage, Aquinas held that because the human will always chooses the good, knowledge of God is dependent on the intellect. Scotus, on the other hand, made the intellect dependent on the human will. Reason, said Scotus, could show that faith is reasonable, could refute objections against it and could encourage inquirers to believe, but it could not demonstrate the truth of Christianity apart from revelation. Others such as William of Ockham (1300-1349) made the same argument for philosophical reasons.

Others rejected even the fetters Aquinas had left on reason, believing that there was functionally nothing to which reason could not speak. For example, Raimundus Sabundus (d. 1436) wrote a volume eventually titled *Natural Theology* that displayed "an exceptional confidence in the power of reason to prove almost the whole of the Christian faith without reliance on the authority of the Bible or Church."[29] Sabundus distinguished what is known from the Bible from what can be known through human reason through "reading" what he called "the book of creatures." The book of creatures is not a written volume but rather the result of human reflection on the nature of reality, goodness and community. Both "books," he held, are fully authoritative and infallible and both attest to the truthfulness of the Christian faith, but the book of creatures holds primacy because no one would accept the Bible unless he was first convinced that God existed and was trustworthy.[30] The Bible becomes necessary only when humans become blind to the results of reason.

The military successes of Muslims in the fourteenth and fifteenth centuries brought about a new round of religious apologetics, much of it very negative in tone. Against Islam, Christian apologists decried inconsistencies in the Qur'an and the hedonism of Islamic eschatology. Against Judaism, Giannozzo Manetti (1396-1459), for example, contrasted the relative sterility of Jewish culture with the cultural fertility of Christianity, which had brought about not only spiritual renewal but also a host of poets, painters, historians and scientists.[31] But not all religious apologists in this period were aggressive and negative. Nicholas of Cusa (1401-1464) wrote a book titled *Sifting the Qur'an,* which instead of refutation, sought to identify and separate the good from the bad in the Qur'an. He attributed Muhammad's rejection of Christianity to the fact that he was only aware of a heretical form of it.[32] He also wrote *On Peace or Concord in the Faith,* a book in which he discussed the concepts that could be held in common by all the major religions, assuming they all made concessions compatible with their conscientious commitments. The dialogue presupposed the truth of the basic outline of the Roman Catholic faith but still acknowledged the value of other religious traditions.[33]

5. THE REFORMATION

The vast majority of the apologetics done during the religiously chaotic period of the Reformation and Counter-Reformation was not really apologetics according to the definition offered in chapter one. As important as the debates between Catholics and Protestant reformers were, they were intramural theological debates between Christians rather than apologetics. Nevertheless, the theological questions debated in the Reformation stimulated a host of apologetic works. That is because there is nothing that encourages apologetic efforts more than well-motivated and pointed objections, whether they be from within or without Christianity. Moreover, both Catholic and Protestant voices in the Reformation saw their arguments as apologetic in nature. While Catholic apologists such as Johann Eck (1486-1543) focused exclusively on the intramural debates of the Reformation, others such as Desiderius Erasmus (1466-1536) and Robert Bellarmine (1542-1621) engaged in apologetics with a broader focus. Similarly, while the early Protestant reformers were clearly focused on developing a theological stance in opposition to the Roman Catholic Church, they nevertheless still developed positions of apologetic significance, particularly with respect to the role of reason in theology and apologetics.

Martin Luther (1483-1546). Martin Luther never developed anything like a formal system of apologetics, primarily because of his view of the relationship between faith and reason. Luther held that prior to faith, reason could only raise objections and engender doubts; it could do nothing to direct one toward spiritual truth.[34] For Luther, human depravity necessitated that all genuine knowledge of God be a gift of grace (*sola gratia*) and that human beings could do nothing, whether ethical works or intellectual exercise, to come to God on their own merits (*sola fidei*). "Reason, thou art foolish," he said. "So the Godly by faith kill such a beast . . . and thereby do offer to God a most acceptable sacrifice and service."[35] Luther also called into question the necessity of rational defenses of the faith: "We must take care not to deface the Gospel, to defend it so well that it collapses. Let us not be anxious: the Gospel needs not our help; it is sufficiently strong of itself. God alone commends it, whose it is."[36]

While some have seen in Luther a complete and unmitigated repudiation of apologetics, others conclude only that he was correcting the excesses of his day. Regardless, Luther's diatribe against the intrusion of philosophy and reason into theology must be seen in light of the excess of confidence in which late medieval theologians combined theology and Aristotelian philosophy. The problem, he said, is thinking that "theology cannot do without Aristotle."[37] His real burden was to make sure that people did not think that they could prove their religious beliefs using reason alone. This is both because human reason is idolatrous and liable to create a god of our liking and because there is a great danger that sinful humans will conclude that what can be known of God on the basis of natural revelation is all that can be known of God.[38]

Luther's close associate and systematizer, Philip Melanchthon (1497-1560), allowed for a far greater role for philosophy and reason than did Luther. Not only did he allow for the exercise of apologetics focused on those who already had embraced the faith, but in his later works he admitted that apologetics could bring the sinful person closer to the gospel by showing him or her that a wise and loving God exists and that he created the world.

John Calvin (1509-1564). While the main purpose of Calvin's teaching was to reform the church, his writings, particularly his magisterial *Institutes of the Christian Religion* (1559), held much by way of apologetic relevance. Unlike Luther, *John Calvin* argued that one who contemplated God's creation could come to knowledge of God's existence, power and goodness. In fact, there are, according to Calvin, no true atheists, for all humans possess the *sensus divinitatis*—an innate sense of God—that makes humans aware of divine reality. This natural knowledge of God is invariably superstitious, idolatrous and self-serving. Consequently, left to their own accord, humans cannot deny God's existence, but they "rob him of his justice and providence, and represent him as sitting idly in heaven."[39] Also unlike Luther, Calvin emphasized— on the first page of the *Institutes*, no less—that "knowledge of God and of ourselves are connected."[40] The two forms of knowledge are "joined by many bonds," and, although they are distinct, they cannot be separated.[41]

With Luther, however, Calvin stressed that the sinfulness of humanity made our attempts at knowledge of God invariably idolatrous. Sinful humans obfuscate the image of the holy God with an idol of their own imagination. The result is that sinful humans are, just as Luther said, unable to prove their religious beliefs using reason alone. Consequently, for Calvin, apologetics, construed as the task of demonstrating the existence of the Christian God to those without faith, was impossible. However, when a person embraces the truth contained in God's special revelation, their idolatrous image is replaced. God repairs the effects of sin on their theological vision with the "spectacles of Scripture." Calvin asserted that just as eyes dimmed with age "when aided with glasses begin to read distinctly, so Scripture, gathering together the impressions of Deity, which, till then, lay confused in their minds, dissipates the darkness, and shows us the true God clearly."[42] Scripture, therefore, was the heart of Calvin's system of apologetics. While, without Scripture, humans warp the *sensus divinitatis* to their own desires and goals, Scripture alone distinguishes God, as creator of the world, from the whole herd of fictitious gods.[43]

While Scripture was for Calvin the starting point for apologetics, it is not a starting point that can be reached through reason. Humans cannot put on the spectacles of Scripture until they receive the inward testimony of the Holy Spirit that vouches for the veracity of Scripture. Moreover, the Spirit must also reform our desires for God; Scripture must be not only revealed to our minds but sealed on our hearts.[44] Consequently, the primary and sufficient reason for embracing the authority of Scripture is not human reason but the inward testimony of the Holy Spirit. In the *Institutes*, Calvin argued:

> Unless this certainty, higher and stronger than any human judgment, be present, it will be in vain to fortify the authority of Scripture by arguments, to establish it by common agreement of the church, or to confirm it with other helps. For unless this foundation is laid, its authority will always remain in doubt. Conversely once we have embraced it devoutly as its dignity deserves, and have recognized it to be above the common sort of things, those arguments—not strong enough before to engraft and fix the certainty of Scripture in our minds—become very useful aids.[45]

To this end, Calvin offered a host of auxiliary proofs of what one already accepts due to the inward work of the Holy Spirit. Such arguments render Scripture fully credible to the human mind who embraces the leading of the Spirit. The truthfulness of Scripture is vouched for by the antiquity of the books of Scripture, the honesty of the writers, publicly attested miracles, and the fulfillment of prophecy and through the preservation of the text of Scripture through history.[46]

One might fruitfully characterize both Luther's and Calvin's views of the role of reason in apologetics with the help of the distinction between the magisterial and ministerial use of reason. When employed in its magisterial function, reason stands over and judges the Christian faith. The arguments of Luther and Calvin against the practice of natural theology are objections to the *magisterial use of reason* they assumed accompanied all attempts to develop a theology apart from Scripture. But both Calvin and Luther acknowledge the *ministerial use of reason*: namely, that reason might fruitfully aid the faithful in their interpretation of Scripture, and in the articulation and defense of the truths found in it.

By the end of the Reformation, Christianity was as polarized as it had ever been, and this polarization was reflected in the practice of apologetics. Not only were there deep divisions on theological matters, but the methodological gulf separating natural theologians like Sabundus and Protestant Reformers like Luther was so deep and wide as to raise the question of whether they were truly defending the same God. Nonetheless, the patristic, medieval and Reformation apologists bequeathed to their descendants a substantial body of apologetic arguments for Christian belief. It was left to the modern world to decide what to do with the contributions of the first 1,500 years of Christian apologetics.

> *Both Calvin and Luther acknowledge the ministerial use of reason: namely, that reason might fruitfully aid the faithful in their interpretation of Scripture, and in the articulation and defense of the truths found in it.*

KEY TERMS

political apologetics
religious apologetics
Justin Martyr
Origen
Augustine
Anselm
Peter the Venerable
Thomas Aquinas
Martin Luther
John Calvin
magisterial use of reason
ministerial use of reason

3

MODERN AND CONTEMPORARY
APOLOGETICS

The previous chapter detailed the history of Christian apologetics up through the tumultuous period of the Reformation. After the Reformation, the tone of Christian apologetics changes in significant ways. This chapter will consider apologetics from the Enlightenment to today, closing with a survey of current trends in apologetics and some suggestions about the shape of Christian apologetics going forward into the twenty-first century.

I. THE ENLIGHTENMENT

In the seventeenth and eighteenth centuries, a period ostentatiously self-labeled "the Enlightenment," there was a great deal of excellent apologetic work. Nevertheless, this period is known as a time when the opponents of orthodox Christian belief began to get the upper hand on Christian apologists. This is partially because Christians—Catholic and Protestant alike—continued to aim many of their arguments at each other and partially because the period of the Renaissance and Reformation made the ground fertile for an explosion of skepticism. There were three reasons for this explosion of skepticism. First, the assumption that human reason was sufficient to demonstrate the whole of Christianity began to wither as it was realized that many of the "proofs" for Christianity could be resisted by a well-motivated skeptic. Second, while the Wars of Religion in the sixteenth and seventeenth centuries were as much about politics as religion, the fact that hundreds of thousands of people were killed over what on the surface seemed to be a theological dispute between Catholics and Protestants decreased the tolerance of many of the survivors for religious fervor of any kind. Finally, with the rise of Protestantism and its emphasis on the priesthood of the believer, the Bible was translated into vernacular languages and widely disseminated. The resulting explosion of heterodox readings of biblical passages was fertile ground for objections to the reliability and authority of Scripture.

In such a context, the apologetic audience changed significantly. While apologetics in the first thousand years of Christianity was taken up with debates between Judaism and Islam, for the first time, the audience of Christian apologetics included those who rejected God's existence (skeptics and freethinkers), those who accepted God's existence but rejected divine revelation (deists), and those who accepted divine revelation but rejected the importance or value of religious belief (libertines).

The *deism* of the Enlightenment stands in a unique place in the history of apologetics. At least some of the deists saw themselves as apologists for Christianity.[1] Their goal was to defend religion against atheism by reducing it to its rational and ethical dimensions. *Lord Herbert of Cherbury* (1583-1648), for example, sought to end the rampant religious strife manifested in the Wars of Religion with a common commitment to reason. Like other deists after him, he held firm to two fundamental ideas: (1) All aspects of religion must be rigorously proved before the bar of reason; those that cannot must be rejected. (2) The chief value of religion is found in providing a foundation for morality. Deists such as Lord Herbert argued not only that their deistic version of Christianity was justifiable but that it was eminently preferable to atheism.

Other deists had no apparent apologetic motives. Their goal was simple: to refute the irrational, supernatural elements of Christianity. Notable among these was *Herman Samuel Reimarus* (1694-1768), a deistic rationalist whose *Apology for or Defense of the Rational Worshipers of God* (most of it published posthumously) was a thoroughgoing attack on the very idea of supernatural revelation and the miraculous. He ridicules the Old Testament and argues that Jesus was a deluded fanatic and that the disciples lied about the resurrection of Jesus and fabricated practically all of New Testament Christianity. Many of his arguments are still used by skeptics today.

> While apologetics in the first thousand years of Christianity was taken up with debates between Judaism and Islam, for the first time, the audience of Christian apologetics included those who rejected God's existence.

Joseph Butler (1692-1752). *Joseph Butler* is one of the best known and most highly respected defenders of Christianity against deism. His *The Analogy of Religion, Natural and Revealed, to the Constitution and Course of Nature* (1736) was designed to refute the deistic claim that the concept of divine revelation is intellectually untenable. Consequently, his apologetic was not designed to prove that Christianity is true, nor was it designed to provide an intellectual framework for the Bible. His goal was to show that the concept of divine revelation is not unreasonable. Accordingly, his argument dealt in probabilities because he averred that for finite humans "probability is the very guide of life."[2] His argument was that "natural religion" (religion based only on reason, not on revelation) is insufficient because it is very reasonable to believe that this life is a probationary period leading up to a time of judgment after death. This life, after all, does not contain perfect justice; there are times when virtue is not rewarded and evil is not punished. One who accepts God's goodness (as deists typically did), therefore, should believe that justice will be meted out in the afterlife. Moreover, he argued that even if there are benefits of a pure natural religion, they are not widely recognized except in contexts where divine revelation has been received. Finally, revelation is necessary, for there is no way that natural religion can uncover the truth that Jesus Christ is savior of the world, which, if true, is crucially important.

Butler also sought to answer objections commonly raised by deists of his day. He did so by pointing out that the deists' objections to revealed religion also applied to their natural religion. In this regard, he contended that the uniqueness of miracles is no argument against their existence because nature itself is full of irregularities and singularities. Similarly, he argued that the lack of universality of revelation was not an argument against its being genuine since nature itself does not reward all people equally. Finally, he answered the objection that God should have given his revelation in a manner that all people would have recognized as indubitable by arguing that God intends his message to be heard only by those who seek honestly and passionately. Deists, he said, cannot object to this arrangement because knowledge of the natural world is similarly affected by motives, passions and prejudices. If this is true of the natural world, why not the religious world?

While Butler's arguments were wholly inadequate against atheists, they did expose the inconsistencies of deists—and that was his goal. Moreover, his method of argumentation was unique, foreshadowing a pair of contemporary apologetic systems: evidentialist and cumulative case apologetics. (More on these apologetic systems in chapter four.)

John Locke (1632-1704). Locke's confidence in the capacity of reason to articulate and defend the Christian faith was profound. In his *An Essay Concerning Human Understanding,* he argued that the existence of God is "the most obvious truth that reason discovers," having an evidence "equal to mathematical certainty."[3] In fact, not only did *John Locke* argue that God's existence could be rationally demonstrated, but he argued that it must be. If Christian beliefs could not be proved by reason, then the Christian faith would be unjustified. While Locke enthusiastically and unhesitatingly accepted the idea of divine revelation, he held that revelation cannot conflict with reason and that, in fact, its authenticity must be guaranteed by rational proofs.

> Revelation is natural reason enlarged by a new set of discoveries communicated by God immediately, which reason vouches the truth of by the testimony and proofs it gives that they come from God. So that he that takes away reason to make way for revelation, puts out the light of both; and does much the same as if he would persuade a man to put out his eyes the better to receive the remote light of an invisible star by a telescope.[4]

It is difficult to underestimate Locke's influence. While there is no doubt that his intentions were sincere, his arguments have been employed equally by subsequent generations of rationalist skeptics and rationalist apologists. Both enthusiastically accepted Locke's requirement that all aspects of religion must be rationally proved; skeptics deemed those proofs to be unsuccessful while rationalist apologists deemed those proofs to be effective.

Not only did John Locke argue that God's existence could be rationally demonstrated, but he argued that it must be.

Henry Dodwell (1700-1742). While his arguments are not spectacular, the approach of *Henry Dodwell* deserves mention, particularly because it stands in such sharp contrast to the approach of John Locke. Among a sea of theological rationalism and evidentialism, Dodwell's work *Christianity Not Founded on Argument* (1642) was unique. Dodwell argued that it is inappropriate to base faith on rational argument, for faith cannot be postponed while reason cautiously weighs evidence and computes probabilities. Faith must be a complete and unwavering commitment. Consequently, the Christian faith lies outside the determination of human reason and is a gift of the Holy Spirit imparted to each individual separately and supernaturally.[5] Dodwell's approach to Christian belief has been taken by some as a repudiation of apologetics, but by others as an affirmation that apologetics must be subjective, existential and personal rather than rational or intellectual. On this latter interpretation, Dodwell anticipated experiential approaches to apologetics that were given forceful explanation a century later by Søren Kierkegaard.

Blaise Pascal (1623-1662). In addition to being a first-rate mathematician and physicist, after his conversion in 1655 *Blaise Pascal* became arguably the best and most influential apologist of the Enlightenment. Pascal's genius was that he incorporated the insights of both Locke and Dodwell into an amazingly balanced and nuanced apologetic. After sharing the gospel with two friends, both avowed freethinkers, Pascal planned to write *An Apology for the Christian Faith*. Sadly, his untimely death left his work unfinished, and all we have of his work is a collection of notes known as the *Pensées*.

Pascal departed from his apologetic predecessors in eschewing almost completely all attempts to prove God's existence. Even if such proofs were valid, they suggested not the God of the Bible, but only an undifferentiated creator. For Pascal, deism was not a significant improvement on atheism. The only God that was the proper object of knowledge was the "God of Abraham, Isaac and Jacob."[6] Instead he asked his interlocutor, a religiously indifferent intellectual, to consider the situation of humans and consider whether any of the religions or philosophical systems gave a plausible account of the state of humanity or offered any hope for the human condition. Pascal found Christianity unique in that while other religions and philosophies emphasized either human greatness or human frailty, only Christianity struck the proper balance between the two. The image of God in humans explained the nobility of human beings, and the fall of humans into sin explained our propensity toward evil. Pascal applied these twin aspects of human nature to the matter of knowledge of God, finding two central truths in the Christian message: (1) There is a God that humans are capable of knowing, and (2) human sinfulness separates us from God and renders our knowledge of God, at best, murky, inchoate and shot through with doubt. These two truths must be held in balance, according to Pascal, for emphasizing the knowledge of God over human sinfulness leads to intellectual pride and arrogance, but emphasizing human sinfulness over knowledge of God leads to despair.[7] Hence Pascal's apologetic was fundamentally christological in its focus, for in Jesus Christ, Pascal found appropriate emphasis on both aspects of the Christian message—God exists and is revealed in Jesus, and humans are sinful and in need of Christ as redeemer.

While God has given humans signs of his existence, he has disguised them so that only those who are truly seeking him with an open and repentant heart will see them—"[in faith] there is enough light for those who only desire to see, and enough obscurity for those who have a contrary disposition."[8] Without that disguise many, even most, people would believe in God, but it would be mere belief and would be devoid of passion or commitment. This would be a problem because, according to Pascal, the passion with which we seek God is an essential part of religious knowledge: "There are two kinds of people one can call reasonable; those who serve God with all their heart because they know him, and those that seek Him with all their heart because they do not know him."[9] While Pascal placed substantial emphasis on the heart, he strove to avoid both of two extremes: "to exclude reason" and "to admit reason only."[10] Hence Pascal's view of the relationship between faith and reason struck a similar chord to Augustine's: the proper function of reason is to aid the heart and will to submit to God. Although faith is not based on arguments, there are, according to Pascal, good arguments for Christianity: the successful establishment of Christianity, the changed lives of Christians, biblical miracles and fulfilled prophecies. These arguments provide confirmation of the claims of Jesus given to humans in the Bible.

For those who find the evidence for and against Christianity equal, Pascal suggested his famous (some might say infamous) "wager." Pascal asked his audience to consider what is gained and lost by either believing or failing to believe in God. If God exists and you believe, there is infinite reward; if God exists and you disbelieve, there is infinite punishment. If God does not exist and you believe, you have a finite loss; if God does not exist and you disbelieve, you have finite gain. Those that do not believe, therefore, face a choice between infinite punishment (if God exists) and finite gain (if he doesn't). Pascal's wager was clearly not a proof of God's existence, and based on other things Pascal said, it is also clearly not an attempt to encourage the unbeliever to believe in God solely for the purpose of avoiding eternal punishment. It is probably best understood as an encouragement for skeptics to take seriously the importance of making a decision. Pascal used this argument to minimize the indifference of his religiously indifferent interlocutor.

Pascal's apologetic is unique in a number of respects. First, Pascal departed from his apologetic predecessors in what he claimed for his apologetic arguments. While he admitted that his arguments fell short of absolute proof, he nonetheless held that they were sufficient to encourage one "to obey the inclination to follow [the Faith]" and that "it is certain that there is no ground for laughing at those who follow it."[11] It is rare even today to find such a balanced approach to religious arguments, and given the rationalism of his day, Pascal's courage and genius are difficult to underestimate. Second, Pascal's approach was way ahead of its time in that it took into account different personality and learning styles. Some people, noted Pascal, are more intuitive in their approach to matters of the faith, others are more mathematical; some desire precision above all else, others focus on comprehension. With this realization, Pascal encouraged an audience-specific approach to apologetics. His goal was to help people discover the truth of Christianity for themselves, for he rightly noted that "people are generally better persuaded by the reasons which they have themselves discovered than by those which have come into the minds of others."[12]

Pascal's approach was way ahead of its time in that it took into account different personality and learning styles.

Despite his genius, Pascal's approach to apologetics was not widely emulated in the years that followed. This is partially because his work was never published in its final form, but primarily because after the Scientific Revolution, and particularly after the findings of Galileo and Sir Isaac Newton revolutionized the way humans viewed their world, most apologists spent the next three centuries seeking to demonstrate the scientific credibility of the Christian faith.[13]

2. THE NINETEENTH CENTURY

Until the Enlightenment, the task of the Christian apologist was relatively easy because the lines between Christian and non-Christian were relatively clear. The growing influence of deism in the Enlightenment, however, blurred those lines significantly. And that trend was to continue through the nineteenth century. The rise of historical biblical criticism, Protestant liberalism and

Catholic modernism all constituted challenges to orthodox Christianity. In this context, Christian scholars began to reflect on the task of apologetics itself—its nature, its relationship to other theological disciplines and its methodology.

During this period there increasingly became two very distinct types of apologetics being practiced. The first—call it *traditional apologetics*—was primarily defensive and sought to respond to the attacks on traditional Christian beliefs; the second—call it *revisionist apologetics*—sought to forge a synthesis between Christianity and secular philosophies with the purpose of demonstrating the relevance of Christianity to cutting-edge intellectual endeavors. To the traditional apologists, revisionist apologists were barely Christian; to revisionist apologists, the arguments of traditional apologists were hopelessly out of date. While my sympathies lie decisively with the traditional apologist's desire to defend orthodox theology, it is important to look at the contribution of the revisionists as well.

Friedrich Schleiermacher (1768-1834). Friedrich Schleiermacher is a pivotal figure in the history of Christian thought. Born into a Moravian pietist home and heavily influenced by the great German philosopher Immanuel Kant (1724-1804), he forged an uneasy alliance between an emphasis on personal relationship of God and an emphasis on reason. His influential synthesis has given him the title the father of modern theology. While his work was theological, he clearly saw his task as apologetic—his *On Religion: Speeches to Its Cultured Despisers* (1799) was an apologetic directed at skeptical intellectuals. Taking a cue from deistic apologists, he took great pains to show that most traditional Christian doctrines can be reinterpreted in ways that do not offend modern sensibilities—miracle, inspiration, prophecy, immortality are all reinvented to avoid their becoming stumbling blocks to his skeptical audience.

Because Schleiermacher accepted Kant's critique of speculative reason, he had no intention of seeking to prove God's existence. Neither was he interested in building an apologetic on Scripture, for he accepted the deistic critique of the concept of divine revelation. His apologetic, therefore, responded to the spiritual poverty of the reason-only approach of the Enlightenment. He said, "Humanity and fatherland, art and science . . . have taken possession of your minds so completely that no room is left over for the eternal and holy being that for you lies beyond the world."[14] In ignoring religion, Schleiermacher's "cultured despisers" had sought to divorce from themselves something absolutely fundamental to human existence, the inner experience of absolute dependence on something ultimate. So that is where Schleiermacher built his case for religion—on the universal sense of absolute dependence. The purpose of religion, he said, is to cultivate this sense of absolute dependence. After dismissing polytheism, he found Christianity superior to both Judaism and Islam. Judaism was too particularistic and was "nearly extinct," and Islam subordinated the moral order to sensuous pleasures. So his apologetic consisted of two steps: (1) Religion is necessary to human life, and (2) Christianity is the best religion.

Schleiermacher was also one of the first figures to think systematically about the task of apologetics itself. He distinguished between apologetics, the task of articulating the essentials of the faith in an intellectually defensible manner, and polemics, the task of detecting and correcting deviations within the Christian community. The first formal, systematic work of apologetics, titled *Christian Apologetics* (1829), was written by Schleiermacher's student Karl Heinrich Sack (1789-1875).[15]

Søren Kierkegaard (1813-1855). Kierkegaard's influence on apologetics is complicated. Some see in *Søren Kierkegaard*, as in Luther before him, an unmitigated assault on the entire apologetic enterprise. And their conclusion is not without evidence. A theme running through all of Kierkegaard's writings is that faith cannot be reached by objective logical thinking. Rational proofs are not only wholly unnecessary for faith; they are, in fact, antithetical to it. When Christianity is reduced to a set of propositions or a set of premises leading to a conclusion, then the personal commitment, passion and purposefulness that must necessarily characterize Christian life is lost. Rational proofs are only necessary when faith loses commitment and passion—when faith ceases to be faith.[16] Kierkegaard said:

> If one were to describe the whole orthodox apologetical effort in one single sentence, but also with categorical precision, one might say that it has the intent to make Christianity plausible. To this one might add that, if this were to succeed, then would this effort have the ironical fate that precisely on the day of its triumph it would have lost everything and entirely quashed Christianity.[17]

Even if rational arguments produced a faith that was factually correct, it would still be problematic because such beliefs lack the degree of belief and strength of commitment that must necessarily accompany Christian belief.

For Kierkegaard, Schleiermacher embodied exactly what was wrong with apologetics. The attempt to make God's existence or the incarnation of God in Jesus Christ plausible to the people of his day inevitably resulted in compromising Christianity. Kierkegaard was writing at a time when nearly everyone professed to be a Christian, but relatively few held their beliefs with the enthusiasm and purposeful clarity of New Testament Christians. He said: "My intention is to make it difficult to become a Christian, yet not more difficult than it is and not difficult for the obtuse and easy for the brainy, but qualitatively and essentially difficult for every human being."[18]

Much of Kierkegaard's work was done under pseudonyms, which was part of his method of "indirect communication." His goal was not to argue for a concept directly but to talk about it in such a way that assisted people to come to the truth on their own terms. In this sense, Kierkegaard's apologetic is similar to Pascal's. The truth of Christianity is seen in the fact that it answers a real human need. In a less Pascalian fashion, however, Kierkegaard argued that the solution offered by Christianity is true precisely because it is absurd according to the expectations and logical standards of human beings. If humans were to make up a religion, it would be a religion robbed of mystery and paradox. Christianity is therefore true because it is so unlike anything that humans would have made up. Therefore, for Kierkegaard, faith is ultimately irrational in human terms. The way beyond sterile objective, logical thinking is passionate subjec-

> *For Kierkegaard, faith is ultimately irrational in human terms.*

tivity. Accordingly, for Kierkegaard, apologetics should not focus on arguments, but on lived experiences.

John Henry Newman (1801-1890). John Henry Newman is widely regarded as one of the most accomplished apologists of his age, especially by Catholics. As a convert to Catholicism, his arguments for the essential truth of Catholicism continue to be widely read and highly valued. While Newman valued rational and historical evidences, he never felt that such evidences were capable of causing unbelievers to commit their lives to Jesus Christ. "No doctrine of the church can be rigorously proved by historical evidence," he said, "but at the same time, no doctrine can be simply disproved by it."[19] Moreover, reason unconstrained by external authority is liable to profound error and even idolatry. Consequently, Newman articulated his apologetics in the form of personal narrative: "In religious enquiry, each of us can speak only for himself, and for himself he has a right to speak. His own experiences are enough for himself, but he cannot speak for others; he cannot lay down the law."[20]

Newman held that people make decisions regarding religious beliefs based on a complex set of attitudes, tastes, preferences, assumptions and way of approaching questions; their decisions are not simply intellectual; they are not motivated purely by logic. Nevertheless, Newman pressed arguments into apologetic service. He argued that the testimony of the human conscience implies the existence of a supreme moral being whose commands alone ground the moral realm. Equally evident is the moral degradation of the world, a feature of reality only explained, said Newman, by an estrangement between humans and their Creator. The universal religious impulse in humans also testifies to the basic human need to reconnect with God in redemption.[21] Finally, Newman offered an impressive probabilistic argument for the truth of Christianity based on the tenacity of theistic belief in Jewish people surrounded by polytheism and the success of the Christian church in fulfilling Jesus' commandment to spread the gospel to the ends of the earth. While this argument falls short of compelling belief, Newman believed that it is sufficient to ground complete confidence in the truth of Christianity.

3. THE TWENTIETH CENTURY

The advent of the twentieth century presented a Christian church that was as divided as it had ever been. The chasm between Catholics and Protestants had deepened because of Vatican I, and the early years of the twentieth century saw the birth of fundamentalism, a pushback against the theological, social and cultural influence of liberal theology. In fact, the pushback against theological liberalism was not limited to conservative Christians. The attempt to build religion on purely rational principles was bearing the fruit of unbelief as Charles Darwin (1809-1882) and his theory of evolution and natural selection helped many of those who would have been deists in the eighteenth century become the skeptics and atheists of the nineteenth century. Consequently, at the advent of the twentieth century, apologetic battle lines were being drawn between Catholics and Protestants, liberals and fundamentalists, Christians and skeptics, and, of course, Christians and members of the other world religions.

Moreover, in the early years of the twentieth century, there were numerous and vociferous debates about the nature of apologetics itself (more on these in chapter 4). The most conspicuous of these occurred between the Old-Princeton School represented by B. B. Warfield (1851-1921) and the Amsterdam School represented by Abraham Kuyper (1837-1920) and Herman Bavinck (1854-1921). The essence of the debate concerned the extent to which human reason could establish some of the fundamental truths of Christianity. Warfield placed the task of apologetics before theology; its function was to establish the grounds on which theology may proceed. Kuyper and Bavinck, on the other hand, placed apologetics after theology, seeing its role not as offensive but as defensive; apologetics is not about providing grounds for theological beliefs but about defending the theological beliefs one already holds.

Karl Barth (1886-1968). Into this context came the most influential theologian of the twentieth century, *Karl Barth.* Barth was not an apologist. In fact, his critique of nineteenth-century apologetics has had a profound and lasting impact. Apologists like Friedrich Schleiermacher, said Barth, go to the world of unbelief "carrying a white flag," and in their attempt to mediate between faith and unbelief, they fail to do justice to the God of the Bible.[22] The Christian God is "wholly other" and, therefore, cannot be approached using human arguments. If humans are to come to knowledge of God, it must be on God's initiative in Jesus Christ, the self-revelation of God. Further, Barth's emphasis on the proclivity of humans to idolatry—"creating God in our image"—led him to assert that humans were not able to choose to follow God. Rather, the only viable response to God's grace is one of obedience, and therefore the best and only apologetic is to present God's revelation as the witness of faith against unbelief. While some have suggested that Barth was opposed to the very concept of defending and commending the faith, such a perspective is deeply mistaken. He was opposed to any and all attempts to come to knowledge of God apart from an acknowledgment of human sinfulness and apart from divine revelation. Such pretensions to theological knowledge amounted to little more than speaking about God by speaking about humanity in a loud voice. Rather, his objection was leveled at approaches to apologetics like Warfield's, approaches that made apologetics a necessary precondition for theology. But from the perspective of God's self-revelation in Jesus, it is possible and desirable to present the faith in a way that is compelling. Theology, said Barth, "has to speak all along the line as faith opposing unbelief, and to that extent all along the line her language must be apologetic."[23] In other words, according to Barth, the best apologetics is good theology.

> *According to Barth, the best apologetics is good theology.*

Clive Staples Lewis (1898-1963). Some might be surprised at the inclusion of *C. S. Lewis* in this brief history. He was, after all, not technically an apologist, theologian or philosopher. By training and vocation, he was a professor of medieval literature. Further, his apologetic writings were almost completely written at a popular level. Even his friend J. R. R. Tolkien somewhat disparagingly referred to Lewis as "everyman's theologian."[24] Further, Lewis acknowledged that he was not a theologian. Instead, he described his work as a "translator," one who rendered Christian doctrine into a language nonspecialists would listen to and could understand. He was also quick to point out, "If real theologians had tackled this laborious work of translation about a hundred years ago, when they began to lose touch with the people (for whom Christ died) there would be no place for me."[25] Whether he be categorized as a theologian or translator, it is impossible to ignore Lewis's contribution to apologetics. In 1980, *Time* magazine labeled him "this century's most-read apologist for God."[26]

Lewis's popularity is undoubtedly at least partially a function of his literary genius. His wit, literary style and clarity of expression are practically unparalleled. Given his literary talents, it is unsurprising that a good bit of Lewis's apologetic was undercover, disguised as works of fiction. Speaking about his three-volume space trilogy and his seven-volume Chronicles of Narnia, he said: "Any amount of theology can now be smuggled into people's minds under cover of romance without their knowing it."[27] Lewis's best-known apologetic work, *Mere Christianity* (1952),[28] was named in a 1993 *Christianity Today* poll as the most influential Christian book apart from the Bible.[29] In it, he offered compelling arguments against both atheism and dualism and presented a case for the uniqueness of the claims of Jesus Christ. He also wrote an impressive defense of the possibility of the miraculous (*Miracles,* 1960) and a widely read response to the problem of evil (*The Problem of Pain,* 1962).

Despite the breadth of his apologetic repertoire, Lewis was uninterested in offering what one might call pragmatic arguments for Christianity. Christianity should be believed, Lewis routinely said, because it is true, not because it makes you happy, healthy, wealthy or popular. Speaking about his own conversion, he said: "I haven't always been a Christian. I didn't go into religion to make me happy. I always knew a bottle of Port would do that."[30] Lewis did, however, develop a powerful argument for Christian belief from the universal sense of longing humans feel. One commentator has suggested that "there probably is no more dominant theme in all of Lewis's writings than this theme of longing."[31] Drawing on Pascal, Lewis held that humans have a "God-shaped hole" in their hearts. This vacuum strongly suggests both the inadequacy of humans without God and the fact that humans have been designed for relationship with God. That fact that you're hungry doesn't mean you will get fed, but it does entail that there is such a thing as food. If we weren't designed to eat, why would we feel hungry? Similarly, he argued, "if we are really the products of a materialistic universe, why is it we don't feel at home in it?"[32]

Cornelius Van Til (1894-1987). Not only is *Cornelius Van Til* among the most influential apologists of the twentieth century, but he is certainly among the most controversial. Strongly influenced by his Calvinistic theology, his apologetic approach has been labeled presuppositionalism. Because the unregenerate human heart is diametrically opposed to accepting the lordship of God, any attempt to base the truth of Christianity on reasons or proofs that could be recognized by the non-Christian on his own terms is, according to Van Til, wholly wrong-headed and doomed to failure. There is, he famously declared, "no neutral common ground" shared by the Christian and the non-Christian.

Because Scripture transcends human reason, its authority cannot be proved by reason alone. Consequently, the authority of Scripture is not something that can be grasped by reason alone; it must be accepted and honored as self-attesting. In other words, in order to appreciate and understand its contents, one must accept what Scripture says about itself—that it is God's Word, reveals the truth about God, and is the only rule of faith and conduct for the Christian. Van Til says: "The self-attesting Christ of Scripture has always been my starting-point for everything I have said."[33]

> If Christ is who he says he is, then all speculation is excluded, for God can only swear by himself. To find out what man is and who God is, one can only go to Scripture. Faith in the self-attesting Christ of the Scriptures is the beginning, not the conclusion of wisdom![34]

If Christ is the starting point, not a conclusion, how then can one offer an apologetic for Christianity? Despite Van Til's claim that the Christian and the non-Christian have fundamentally different presuppositions and that those presuppositions dramatically affect the way humans view every aspect of life, he still believed that a rational argument for Christianity was both possible and necessary. Those who emphasize evidence and reason, he said, "were quite right in stressing the fact that Christianity meets every legitimate demand of reason. Surely Christianity is not irrational. To be sure, it must be accepted on faith, but surely it must not be taken on blind faith."[35]

The fundamental apologetic challenge, according to Van Til, was "How do you argue with someone who has fundamentally different presuppositions?" His answer: by using a transcendental argument, an argument that seeks to demonstrate that certain presuppositions are necessary for the possibility of rationality. While the Christian and non-Christian accept different presuppositions, Van Til argued that only the Christian's presuppositions allow for genuine rationality and only Christian presuppositions make sense of what we see and experience. Non-Christian presuppositions are ultimately self-defeating. Therefore, for Van Til, faith is based not on reason, but on the fact of God's existence. In fact, reason is absolutely dependent on faith. He said: "I hold that belief in God is not merely as reasonable as other belief; or even a little or infinitely more probably true than other belief; I hold rather that unless you believe in God you

> *For Van Til, faith is based not on reason, but on the fact of God's existence.*

can logically believe in nothing else."[36] Van Til's transcendental argument is, of course, not a direct argument for Christianity, but a *reductio ad absurdum* for the non-Christian's position, an argument that demonstrates the absurd conclusions entailed by all non-Christian worldviews.

Richard Swinburne (b. 1934). The British philosopher, *Richard Swinburne* represents the polar opposite of Van Til's apologetic approach. Swinburne has devoted himself to developing arguments for God's existence, many of them quite impressive. He has written *The Coherence of Theism* (1977), *The Existence of God* (1979) and *Faith and Reason* (1981), and from 1989 to 1998, he published a series of four books defending Christian understandings of atonement, revelation, God's nature, and providence and evil. His stated goal is to "use the criteria of modern natural science, analysed with the careful rigour of modern philosophy, to show the meaningfulness and justification of Christian theology."[37] Some of his most impressive arguments are refutations of various claims that the very concept of God is incoherent and that religious language is either meaningless or hopelessly confused. Swinburne's argument for God's existence proceeds by way of an "inference to the best explanation." After considering the traditional arguments for God's existence, the phenomenon of religious experience and the simplicity of theism as compared to rival worldviews, he argues that the belief that God exists "explains everything we observe, not just some narrow range of data,"[38] and, consequently, the existence of God is "significantly more probable than not."[39]

Alvin Plantinga (b. 1932). Standing between the approaches of Van Til and Swinburne is one of the most influential philosophers of the twentieth century. One commentator has even described *Alvin Plantinga* as the "greatest philosopher of the last century."[40] While Plantinga has written extensively in the fields of metaphysics, epistemology and philosophy of religion, it is clear that all of his writing has been apologetically motivated. He says: "The main function of apologetics is to show that from a philosophical point of view, Christians and other theists have nothing for which to apologize."[41]

Plantinga acknowledges that there are many good arguments

for God's existence and has even developed what some view as the most successful version of the ontological argument. And Plantinga avers that theistic arguments can be "useful aids" in a variety of ways: "They can confirm and support belief reached in other ways; they may move fence-sitters closer to Christian belief; they can function as defeater-defeaters; and they can reveal interesting and important connections."[42] However, he holds that such arguments are not necessary for faith. Following John Calvin, Plantinga defines faith as a "firm and certain knowledge" and sees it as a gift given by the Holy Spirit.[43] Therefore, while one might have interesting arguments for what one believes by faith, Plantinga absolutely rejects what he terms the *evidentialist objection* to belief in God—the notion that belief in God is irrational unless there is a logically adequate argument for God's existence. The evidentialist objection is deeply flawed, says Plantinga, because it makes knowledge of God something only the learned can attain—something contrary to Matthew 5:8: "Blessed are the pure in heart, for they will see God." Moreover, if applied universally, the evidentialist objection renders us unable to rationally accept many beliefs that seem obvious to us, such as the world having been in existence for longer than ten minutes and that other people have minds. Consequently, Plantinga is quick to state that not being able to prove, show or demonstrate God's existence is not a problem since "very little of what we believe can be 'demonstrated' or 'shown.'"[44] In effect, Plantinga severs the link between "having a proof" and "having knowledge of the truth"—it is possible to have the latter without the former.

In addition to his work refuting the evidentialist objection to belief in God, Plantinga is widely credited (even by some atheists) with giving the first philosophically adequate response to the logical problem of evil—the objection to Christianity that says that given the existence of evil, God's existence is logically impossible. While he does not attempt to explain why God allows evil, his free will defense does demonstrate that there is no logical contradiction in God's being perfectly good and all-powerful and his creating human beings who use their free will to bring about evil.[45]

4. LOOKING BACK AND LOOKING FORWARD

As we have seen, every historical context brings certain apologetic advantages and certain apologetic disadvantages. When Christianity is under attack, apologetics becomes part of the fabric of Christian life. In the patristic period, even the deaths of the martyrs took on apologetic overtones. But when Christianity is under attack, there is an unfortunate tendency on the part of Christian apologists to make their job easier by accommodating aspects of the Christian faith to the culture and worldview of Christianity's attackers. Such a revisionist apologetic, even if successful in some sense of the word, has been rightly lambasted by Karl Barth and others. On the other hand, when Christianity is flourishing, the sense of urgency driving apologetics diminishes sharply. When Christianity is part of the air that people breathe (as it was in the Middle Ages), there is relatively less opportunity for apologetics, and the apologetics that occurs is generally of less quality. Moreover, in such a situation, the Christian apologist is often handicapped by a less than adequate understanding of the belief system of his or her interlocutor. Finally, when Christianity is in a place of cultural dominance, Christians apologists have had the unfortunate tendency of turning their apologetic efforts inward and attacking the theology of fellow Christians. Despite these disadvantages, when Christianity is flourishing, there are greater opportunities to develop comprehensive and academically rigorous apologetic arguments. The trick for the apologist in each age and each context is to maximize the advantages of their context without falling prey to the disadvantages—something that is much easier said than done.

In the last 150 years, Christians apologetics has been under a cloud. The draconian excesses and revisionism of rationalist apologists of the eighteenth and nineteenth centuries coupled with the anti-intellectualist retreat of fundamentalism from contact with secular society have done damage to the reputation of Christian apologetics. On this matter, Avery Dulles notes that "the reputation of apologetics reached its nadir when Barth's influence was at its height—that is to say from about 1920 to 1950."[46] But that is, happily, not the end of the story, for Dulles goes on to say that "since the 1950s, particularly among the younger Protestant theologians, there have been some indications that apologetics may be experiencing a revival."[47] This revival as been particularly strong among evangelicals in North America. In fact, Schubert Ogden has said that "the safest generalization regarding Protestant theology since World War II is that it has evidenced a growing concern with its inescapable apologetic task."[48] Contemporary apologists such as William Lane Craig, J. P. Moreland, Peter Kreeft, John Frame, James Sire, Richard Swinburne, Alvin Plantinga and many others are doing an impressive job shouldering his important task.

The trick for the apologist in each age and each context is to maximize the advantages of their context without falling prey to the disadvantages.

But Christian apologists must not assume that the gains of the future will be achieved in the same manner as in the past. Just as there is a tendency on the part of old generals to prepare to win the previous generation's war, Christian apologists must continue to adapt the unchanging message of Christianity to the ever-changing cultural and intellectual milieu if these gains are to continue. To this end, I will offer some suggestions for the shape of Christian apologetics going forward into the twenty-first century. This is, of course, difficult. Speaking about the past is much easier because one has the benefit of hindsight. Nonetheless, I will close this chapter with a brief discussion of three current and future issues in the field of apologetics.

Objections to apologetics. Anti-apologetic movements will continue and perhaps intensify, fueled by wounds from the past mistakes of apologetics that have not fully healed, partially because even today some apologists insist on reopening those wounds by making the same mistakes. The pushback against apologetics will not, as some have said, be a function of our "religiously pluralistic context," for as we have seen, religious pluralism has always been an impetus to apologetic work. Rather, anti-apologetic efforts in the future will arise out of a particular understanding of what is entailed by religious diversity. Fueled by certain strands of thought increasingly popular in Western culture, it will continue to be mistakenly assumed that the assertion of a particular position is inherently intolerant to those with whom you disagree and that arguing for your religious belief and against others exhibits a lack of respect for the views of others. Christians must continue to expose the problems with this line of thinking and continue to defend the appropriateness and importance of the apologetic task. Christians must continue to take seriously the phenomenon of unbelief (by those outside the faith) and doubt (by those inside the faith) and continue to grapple with the concepts and objections that lead to unbelief and doubt. And it is crucially important that Christian apologists do all of this in a humble, Christlike manner.

Postmodernism. The concept of postmodernity is less than clear, and therefore it should not be surprising that postmodernity is something of a mixed blessing for apologetics. Some decry its flirtations with relativism as anathema to apologetics; others herald its deconstruction of the unrealistic standards for rational belief set by modernity. Whatever it is, it will continue to be both a blessing and a curse for Christian apologetics well into the next century. The task for the Christian apologist regarding postmodernism must be one of interaction; nothing is to be gained by pretending it does not exist. Rather, Christians must seek to articulate pictures of truth, rationality and knowledge that acknowledge the postmodern critique of the excesses of modernity. At the same time, they must remain faithful to the Christian concept of God as an objective reality, not merely a social construct, and human knowledge of God and his expectations of humans as possible even if not complete or final.

The globalization of Christianity. With rare exceptions, introductory books on apologetics have largely ignored this issue.[49] However, the rapid globalization of Christianity will pose unique challenges for Christian apologetics in the coming century. Christian apologetics has thus far been defined by and largely practiced by Christians in the Western world. With large increases in the number of Christians in Asia, Africa, and South and Latin America (around 23,000 per day) and substantial declines in the number of Christians in Europe and North America (around 7,600 per day), this will have to change.[50] If Christian apologists fail to acknowledge the import of the globalization and multiculturalization of Christianity, they will restrict their contribution to Christ's kingdom to an increasingly small minority of Christ's followers. Of course, this does not mean that everything done by Western theologians and apologists is mistaken or culturally compromised. Rather, it means that Christian apologists—Western and non-Western alike—must begin to ask the difficult questions regarding the contextualization of the defense of the gospel in non-Western settings. We must strip away the accretion of Western culture while remaining faithful to the uniqueness and cen-

> The rapid globalization of Christianity will pose unique challenges for Christian apologetics in the coming century.

trality of God's self-revelation in Jesus Christ. Christians in all cultures must submit to God's revelation and allow it to control our thoughts and actions, even when it is not particularly palatable to currently fashionable trends, tastes and values.[51]

KEY TERMS
deism
Lord Herbert of Cherbury
Herman Samuel Reimarus
Joseph Butler
John Locke
Henry Dodwell
Blaise Pascal
traditional apologetics
revisionist apologetics
Friedrich Schleiermacher
Søren Kierkegaard
John Henry Newman
Karl Barth
C. S. Lewis
Cornelius Van Til
Richard Swinburne
Alvin Plantinga
evidentialist objection

4

VARIETIES OF APOLOGETICS

As the previous two chapters on the history of apologetics have demonstrated, there are clearly many different perspectives on how Christian apologetics should be done. Moreover, these differences have become more pronounced since the nineteenth century, when apologetics became formalized as a discipline. The task of this chapter is to discuss the different schools of apologetics, why they exist, and what arguments are given for and against each of them.

I. WHY ARE THERE SO MANY DIFFERENCES?

At first blush it might seem surprising that there are so many different and incompatible ways in which apologetics is done. Why is there such a vast gulf standing between the approach of Aquinas and Luther, Locke and Kierkegaard, Barth and Schleiermacher, and Van Til and Swinburne? After all, each is defending the same God, reading the same Scripture, and appealing to the same evidences and reasons, right? Not necessarily. In the last chapter, we briefly discussed revisionist apologists who simply reject many traditional Christian beliefs, including traditional accounts of God's nature and the nature of Scripture. But even among traditional apologists—those who desire to defend orthodox Christian beliefs—there are significant differences in apologetic method. Why is this?

The answer lies (at least partially) in the range of possible answers that might be given to a series of fundamental questions. These questions have been called *meta-apologetic questions* since they are questions about the "methods, concepts, and foundations of apologetic systems and perspectives."[1] I will briefly discuss five such questions, the first three of which are theological in nature.

What is the relationship between faith and reason? From Augustine's time until today this question has preoccupied Christian theologians and apologists who have desired to explain what is involved in the Christian's belief in and commitment to God. Do we start with faith and only then try to explain and justify it? Or do we provide reasons for Christianity and only then, on the basis of those reasons, commit in faith? There is, of course, a continuum of possible answers to this question (see figure 1).

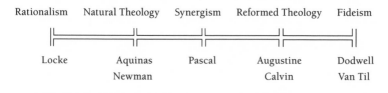

Rationalism	Natural Theology	Synergism	Reformed Theology	Fideism
Locke	Aquinas	Pascal	Augustine	Dodwell
	Newman		Calvin	Van Til

Figure 1. A continuum: The relationship between faith and reason

John Locke represents the position known as *rationalism,* the assertion that reason is the sole arbiter of truth and that faith is unnecessary when rational arguments are present. Thomas Aquinas and John Henry Newman ably represent the tradition of *natural theology,* a position that places primacy on reason but reserves an important role for faith for providing certitude for those unable to formulate theistic arguments or for providing the boundaries in which reason ought to function. *Reformed theology* reverses the primacy, giving faith the principal role. Augustine and John Calvin both held that arguments for the faith are truly valuable, but only for those who have already embraced faith and have received the regenerating work of the Holy Spirit. At the opposite end of the continuum from rationalism, the *fideism* of Henry Dodwell and Cornelius Van Til sharply delimits the use of rational arguments in apologetics, albeit for different reasons—Dodwell because arguments do not provide the level of certainty required for faith and Van Til because sinful humans must accept the authority of Scripture before they can understand arguments for its truthfulness. Finally, between natural and Reformed theology lies *synergism,* a position that gives universal primacy to neither reason nor faith. In some contexts and for some people, reason will lead; in others contexts and for other people, faith. Moreover, faith is absolutely reasonable, and utilizing one's reason is, in an important sense, an act of faith. While Pascal admits that the primary truths of Christianity cannot be proved by reason, he avers that it is reason that shows humanity this fact. And responding to Christ in faith, for Pascal, is the most reasonable thing a person can do.

The question of the *relationship between faith and reason* is closely related to a series of questions regarding the relationship between the Christian faith and nontheological disciplines. Can the Christian apologist benefit from studying philosophy, or understanding scientific discoveries, or considering historical evidences for biblical events? Most Christians have said yes, but some have argued that these disciplines contain presuppositions that are incompatible with the Christian faith. And even those who grant that there is some benefit to studying these disciplines acknowledge that some schools of philosophy or some scientific theories are problematic and need to be contested by the Christian apologist.

To what extent can humans understand God's nature? Closely connected with the previous meta-apologetic question is a question concerning the extent to which human language and thought can be said to "refer" to God. Of course, no one holds that the finite human mind can fully comprehend God's nature. As finite beings, we likely cannot fully cognize anything, much less a being like God. Moreover, most Christians acknowledge that sin affects not only our relationship with God and our moral decisions, but how we think. But, even given our finitude and sinfulness, some hold that partial *knowledge* of God is possible.

> As finite beings, we likely cannot fully cognize anything, much less a being like God.

There are two versions of this question. The first concerns the effect of sin on the mind of the unbeliever, one who has not been regenerated by the Holy Spirit, and the second concerns the effect of sin on the mind of the believer. The more one emphasizes the negative effects of sin on the mind of the unbeliever, the more likely one will be suspicious of the effectiveness of proactive apologetics—rational arguments designed to demonstrate the truth of Christianity. And the more one sees the sin as affecting not only the unbeliever but the believer as well, the more likely one will be suspicious of the effectiveness of all rational arguments, even responsive apologetics—rational arguments designed to defend the Christian faith from objections.

Some question whether humans could understand God even if sin was not a factor. The emphasis Karl Barth places on God's being "wholly other," for example, suggests that even if the noetic effects of sin were not a problem, Barth would still be highly suspicious of using human logic to demonstrate God's existence and nature. Others have a more optimistic view, believing that the fact that God created humans to be in relationship with him entails that he would have created humans with the ability to understand certain fundamental things about his nature—his goodness, love and existence, for example. Such a perspective opens up the possibility for meaningful understanding of God's nature and therefore potentially persuasive arguments regarding his being or existence.

Related to this matter is the question of whether the famous theistic arguments actually work. A very few view the arguments for God's existence as proofs. If you understand the argument, failing to believe is irrational. Many see them as logically valid, but not logically irresistible. That is, there is nothing logically wrong with the arguments, but one or more of the premises of the arguments are such that they can be logically rejected. Others go so far as to reject the arguments as logically fallacious.

3 *What is the role of the Holy Spirit in apologetics?* This question is profoundly important in theology as well as in apologetics. Some see the primary role of the Holy Spirit as preparing the heart of unbelievers for apologetic encounters, others see the Holy Spirit as directing our attention to whom we should speak, and still others see the Holy Spirit as helping unbelievers to get from believing in God to committing themselves to God. Finally, some see the Holy Spirit as causally directing the entire process and see our contribution as minimal. Our basic task is to present the gospel and stay out of the way of the working of the Spirit. Many who see a profound role for the Holy Spirit will demand a diminished role for apologetic arguments. But it is important to see that this is not a zero-sum game. It is possible to see the apologist as significantly involved and still hold that the Holy Spirit will determine the effectiveness of our efforts.

In addition to these three theological questions, one's apologetic method will be affected by the following two philosophical meta-apologetic questions.

1 *What is the nature of truth?* As discussed in the first chapter, apologetics is the defense of the truthfulness of the Christian worldview. But what is truth? Most Christian apologists have un-

derstood truth as a quality or property of statements (or propositions). A statement possesses the quality or property of being true
if it accurately represents the aspect of reality it is trying to describe. My statement "My laptop's battery is depleted" is true if
and only if that particular state of affairs is real. There are, of
course, many nuances that need to be added, but that is the typical picture of truth, usually called the *correspondence theory of
truth*. Some, however, have attempted to deny the correspondence
theory and have sought to replace it with pragmatic utility (beliefs
are true if they are useful), coherence (beliefs are true if they are
coherent or logically fit with a larger body of beliefs or facts), or
personal embodiment (beliefs are not best thought of as true or
false; truth is personal, i.e., Jesus is the truth). Still others have felt
obliged by what some consider the implications of postmodernism to dispense with the concept of truth completely. While I will
consider these matters in greater depth in the final chapters of
this book, for our purposes now, it is sufficient to point out that
the theory of truth one embraces will have significant effects on
one's apologetic method. After all, if one rejects truth, one must
also reject the notion that views
contrary to your own are wrong. In
such a state, arguments for your
position and against other positions are out of place at best (and
ludicrous at worst). In either case,
apologetics ceases to be a viable
enterprise.

> The theory of truth one
> embraces will have
> significant effects on one's
> apologetic method.

2. *What is the task of apologetics?* The answer to this question
may appear obvious, but it is not. Differences in how this question is answered account for a good bit of the differences between apologetic systems. Consider three different answers.
First, one might see the task of apologetics as demonstrating the
rationality of Christian belief. If so, then arguments against ob-

jections to Christian belief and for its reasonability will be the primary tools of the apologist. Second, some construe the task of apologetics as demonstrating that Christian belief is true. Apologists with such an understanding must give arguments not only for the reasonableness of Christianity but also against other rival worldviews. Moreover, if the apologist deems arguments insufficient to demonstrate the truthfulness of Christianity, he or she may argue that the truthfulness of Christianity must be accepted or presupposed rather than argued for. Finally, one might see the task of apologetics as demonstrating that one ought to commit one's life to Jesus Christ. If so, while arguments may be important, they will be only part of the picture. Since it is possible to accept the truth of the Christian worldview but fail to commit one's life to Christ, it will be necessary to go beyond arguments for Christianity to personal appeals or pragmatic considerations in an attempt to make the person aware of his or her need for Christ.

2. DIFFERENT WAYS OF CATEGORIZING APOLOGETIC SYSTEMS

In the two hundred years (or so) that Christians have been thinking systematically about the nature and methodology of apologetics, there have been a number of attempts to categorize the different types of approaches to apologetics. For those engaged in this task, it has been tempting to divide apologetic systems into precise, mutually exclusive categories. Such a categorization, however, has proved to be problematic. Any neat division into, for example, apologetics systems that place a high value on human reason versus those that do not will place diametrically opposed apologetic systems in the same category. The best approach is to allow numerous categories, acknowledging that there will be overlap between these categories.[2]

There have been a variety of ways used to talk about the differences between apologetic systems.[3] *Bernard Ramm*, for example, distinguishes three "families" of apologetic systems: (1) systems that stress the uniqueness of the Christian experience of grace, (2) systems that stress natural theology as the point at which apologetics begins and (3) systems that stress revelation as the foundation upon which apologetics must be built.[4] The strengths of Ramm's approach are many. Grace, natural theology and revelation are undoubtedly absolutely fundamental concepts for any apologetic system. Nevertheless, some have objected that Ramm's system is not "fine-grained" enough.[5] His system does not, some claim, take into account the real and important differences within his apologetic families. For example, even within the family of apologetics that stresses revelation as the foundation upon which apologetics must be built, there are significant differences in explaining why revelation must be the foundation for apologetics. Similarly, within the family that emphasizes natural theology, there are profound differences in how such arguments are used and what is understood as a successful argument.

Another important taxonomy of apologetic systems has been developed by *Gordon Lewis*.[6] He distinguishes different apologetic systems or methods according to their religious epistemology—that is, according to their beliefs about how one acquires religious knowledge. Using this approach, Lewis suggests that there are six different "apologetic systems": (1) pure empiricism (J. Oliver Buswell), (2) rational empiricism (Stuart Hackett), (3) rationalism (Gordon H. Clark), (4) biblical authoritarianism (Cornelius Van Til), (5) mysticism (Earl E. Barrett) and (6) verificationism (E. J. Carnell). There are, of course, profound philosophical differences among these six religious epistemologies. For example, the empirical approach of J. Oliver Buswell leads him to build arguments for the Christian faith on observations of the world—the design of nature and historical evidences for Jesus' life death and resurrection. These arguments, Buswell suggests, will lead the rational, objective observer to accept the truth of Christianity. Van Til obviously is adamantly opposed to any such approach, demanding obedient acceptance of the authority of the Christ of Scripture before the truth of Christianity can be understood. As helpful as Lewis's taxonomy is in many respects, it has two substantial drawbacks. First, appreciating the differences among the different apologetic systems requires a fairly substantial amount of philosophical training, something that most Christians lack, even many of those interested in apologetics. Second, while there are philosophical differences between, for example, pure empiricism and rational empiricism, it is unclear that these philosophical differences mirror differences in apologetic methodology.

Despite the strengths of Ramm's and Lewis's taxonomies (and, undoubtedly, because of their weaknesses), another method of describing apologetic systems has become more commonly used. This method categorizes apologetic systems by their primary argumentative strategy.[7] Even here, there are differences in terminology and classification. Norman Geisler and Steve Cowan each offer five views, but their lists overlap only on three views: classical apologetics, evidentialist apologetics and presuppositional apologetics.[8] Kenneth Boa, on the other hand, suggests four views: classical apologetics (with a rationalist focus), evidentialism (with an empirical focus), Reformed apologetics (with an authoritarian approach) and fideism (with an intuitive approach).[9] Finally, David Clark employs the same four views as Boa (with different titles) but offers a second class of views, one with a person-centered approach rather than a content-centered approach.[10] My own taxonomy of apologetic

> *My own taxonomy of apologetic systems is informed by the conviction that there are three broad argumentative strategies.*

systems is informed by the conviction that there are three broad argumentative strategies: the *evidentialist strategy* (which emphasizes a variety of rational arguments), the *presuppositionalist strategy* (which emphasizes the authoritative testimony of Scripture) and the *experientialist strategy* (which, not surprisingly, emphasizes experience).

3. THE EVIDENTIALIST STRATEGY

As its name indicates, the hallmark of *evidentialism* is its emphasis on rational arguments and evidences. The evidentialist is committed to three ideas. First, since human beings have been created as rational beings and cannot commit themselves to what they believe to be false, rational and evidential arguments for the faith are a crucial element of an apologetic for Christianity. Second, there are profound intellectual objections to the faith that require a well-reasoned, well-supported response. Third, rational and evidential arguments can be very effective in overcoming people's objections to the faith and, at times, in encouraging people to take a step of faith itself. Evidentialists commonly offer C. S. Lewis as the poster child for the success of evidentialist apologetics. Lewis likened his conversion to the return of a prodigal "brought in kicking, struggling, resentful, and darting his eyes in every direction for a chance of escape."[11] While it is unreasonable to see Lewis's conversion as exclusively evidentially motivated, it is undoubtedly true that rational arguments played a substantial role.

Evidentialist apologetics needs to be distinguished from evidentialism, a position that involves the claim that one who accepts a belief without basing it on arguments is irrational. W. K. Clifford gave this view its classic expression saying, "It is wrong, always, everywhere, and for anyone to believe anything upon insufficient evidence."[12] While all evidentialist apologists embrace the apologetic value of rational arguments and evidences, only some of them aver that evidences and arguments are necessary for rational belief in God and that one who accepts a religious belief without basing it on arguments is irrational.

There are other ways of distinguishing among evidentialists. While all evidentialists embrace rational evidences as their primary argumentative strategy, not all use evidence in the same way. In fact, I will identify three different schools within the evidentialist family tree. Some go so far as to label these as separate apologetic systems. I do not do so because I believe that it is clear that their family resemblance is far more significant than their differences.

Classical apologetics. So called because of its ancient pedigree, the defining characteristic of the classical apologetic method is its *two-step approach.* The *classical apologist* argues, first, for the existence of God and, second, that Christianity is the most reasonable form of theism. Such a two-step approach is necessary, claims the classical apologist, because it is ludicrous to argue about which God exists when it has not been established that any God exists. Similarly, appeals to fulfilled prophecies or miracles are ineffective apart from the assumption that a God exists to reveal prophecies or act miraculously.[13] Classical apologists typically make ample use of a wide variety of theistic arguments as well as historical evidences for the reliability of Scripture and the reality of the resurrection of Jesus Christ. Noted contemporary classical apologists include William Lane Craig, Norman Geisler and R. C. Sproul.

Historical apologetics. While *historical apologists* share the classical apologist's emphasis on rational and evidential arguments, they dispute the necessity of arguing for God's existence prior to employing historical arguments from miracles or fulfilled prophecy. According to the historical apologist, historical evidences are sufficient to demonstrate the truthfulness of both Christianity and theism. After all, if one is persuaded of the truthfulness of the resurrection story, included in that commitment is a belief in the existence of a miracle-working deity. Consequently, historical apologetics is labeled a *one-step approach*. A common historical apologetic approach is to use historical evidences to demonstrate the historicity of the New Testament, including the historicity of the miracles of Christ, especially the resurrection. Or a historical apologist might argue that the historical details of the resurrection are explicable only if a God like that described by Christianity actually exists. Contemporary historical apologists include Gary Habermas, Josh McDowell and John Warwick Montgomery.

Cumulative-case apologetics. Those preferring a *cumulative-case approach* to apologetics share the emphasis on rational arguments and evidences held by the classical and evidentialist apologists but insist on neither a one-step nor a two-step approach. Rather, the cumulative-case method might be called a *many-step approach* because it involves piecing together a series of converging arguments and evidences that, taken together, form a hypothesis that (it is claimed) is superior in explanatory power to any of its competitors. Cumulative-case arguments could be used to demonstrate the reasonableness of Christian theism taken as a whole or to explain the reasonableness of a particular Christian doctrine, such as the bodily resurrection of Jesus Christ. Contemporary cumulative-case apologists include William Abraham, Paul Feinberg and Richard Swinburne.

4. THE PRESUPPOSITIONALIST STRATEGY

Presuppositional apologetics is substantially different from the evidentialist strategy. Typically coming from a Reformed or Calvinist theological tradition, presuppositionalists are leery of any attempt to appeal to a common ground with the non-Christian—shared concepts or premises, a shared method of arguing, or shared experiences—holding that such attempts to build on common ground with the non-Christian do not take seriously enough the corruption of all worldviews or systems of thought that do not place the

Christian God and his revelation at the center. In other words, according to the presuppositionalist, the problem with the non-Christian is not a lack of good reasons but innate sinfulness manifested as rebellion against God, a rebellion that first and foremost amounts to a refusal to acknowledge God's proper place. Consequently, the authority of Scripture and of Jesus Christ must be presupposed before sense can be made of arguments for the truthfulness of Christianity. Presuppositionalism is, therefore, sometimes labeled a *no-step apologetic approach,* for there are no argumentative steps that lead directly to the conclusion of the truthfulness of Christianity.

> Presuppositionalists are leery of any attempt to appeal to a common ground with the non-Christian.

Generally speaking, if the hallmark of evidentialism is an appeal to reasons or arguments, presuppositionalism is an appeal to authority. There are, however, differences among presuppositionalists on how that appeal to authority is articulated. Consequently, as with evidentialism, there are a variety of presuppositionalists.[14]

Revelational presuppositionalism. The best-known and most influential variety of presuppositionalism is the *revelational presuppositionalism* of Cornelius Van Til. As briefly discussed in chapter three, Van Til's approach replaces standard arguments and evidences for Christianity with a transcendental argument designed to show that the biblical God is necessary to all claims of meaning or intelligibility. Truth, logic, meaning and value can exist only on the presupposition that the Christian God exists. This argument is not a direct argument for Christianity but a *reductio ad absurdum* for the non-Christian's position, an argument that demonstrates the absurd conclusions entailed by all non-Christian worldviews. Van Til's standard has been ably taken up by his students Greg Bahnsen and John Frame.

Rational presuppositionalism. A staunch opponent of revelational presuppositionalism, Gordon H. Clark (1902-1985) ascribed a much higher value to logical arguments than did Van Til. Because he remained a presuppositionalist, however, Clark maintained one must accept the starting points or axioms of Christianity—that "what the Bible says, God has spoken."[15] As in geometry, axioms are never deduced but are assumed without proof, but Clark asserts that one can know that Christianity is true because it alone is logically consistent and all competing worldviews or philosophies are logically inconsistent. Clark's well-known student, Carl F. H. Henry (1913-2003), also championed this brand of presuppositionalism, *rational presuppositionalism.*

Practical presuppositonalism. A final variety of presuppositionalism is the *practical presuppositonalism* of Francis Schaeffer (1912-1984). While Schaeffer himself avoided being labeled as any particular type of apologist, preferring to be called an evangelist, many have seen Schaeffer's apologetic as presuppositionalist in nature. His apologetic emphasizes the necessity of starting from fundamental Christian truths rather than arguing to them, and he emphasizes the logical inconsistency of all non-Christian worldviews. Unlike both Van Til and Clark, however, Schaeffer argues that all non-Christian worldviews are ultimately unlivable. In so doing, his approach bears some affinities to the next and final apologetic strategy, the experientialist strategy.

5. THE EXPERIENTIALIST STRATEGY

Like presuppositional apologists, *experiential apologists* do not rely on logical arguments or evidences, but their reasons for rejecting an exclusively rational approach is different. They do not hold that the truth of Christianity must be presupposed; rather they hold that it must be experienced. Consequently, while the experiential apologists do not offer outward, logical evidences for the non-Christian to believe, they do offer internal, subjective reasons. For this reason, experiential apologetics might also be termed a one-step approach, although this one step is experiential, not logical.

While religious experience is central to experiential apologetics, it is important to distinguish between arguments for God's existence based on religious experience and experiential apologetics. Some who make apologetic use of religious experiences are not experiential apologists. For example, Richard Swinburne (an evidentialist) has developed detailed arguments for theistic belief based on religious experience.

One type of argument commonly employed by experiential apologists is called the argument *from* religious experience. This argument draws attention both to the universality of religious experiences and to the unique intensity of mystical experiences. Such experiences, it is claimed, are sufficient to suggest the existence of a source of those experiences. Another kind of argument might be called the argument *to* religious experience. This argument calls attention to the transformative powers of the Christian life. The Christian philosopher William Alston explains this eloquently:

> The final test of the Christian scheme comes from trying it out in one's own life, testing the promises the scheme tells us God has made, following the way enjoined on us by the Church and seeing whether it leads to the new life of the Spirit. Admittedly, it is not always clear exactly what this involves; it is not always clear whether we are satisfying the conditions laid down for entering the kingdom; it is not always clear where we are at a given moment in our pilgrimage, whether, for example, an apparent setback or regression is part of the master plan or a failure on our part. And then there is the inconvenient fact that not all members of the

body of Christ agree as to just what is required and just how
the payoff is to be construed. But with all this looseness and
open texture, the fact remains that over the centuries count-
less Christians who have set out to follow the way have found
in their lives that the promises of God have been fulfilled,
that their lives have been different, not 100 percent of the
time and not as quickly and dramatically as they may have
wished, but unmistakably and in the direction the tradition
predicts.[16]

A final kind of experiential argument, articulated with impressive force by Pascal, Søren Kierkegaard and C. S. Lewis, might be
called the argument from nonreligious experience. Drawing on
Pascal, Lewis has given this argument its most famous expression,
asserting that there is a "God-shaped hole" in the heart of every
human being. Apart from God, humans flounder in their effort to
find happiness and meaning in life. Only in a relationship with God
can humans find true joy, ultimate meaning and clear purpose.

6. AN EVALUATION OF THE TRADITIONAL APOLOGETIC SYSTEMS

For a variety of theological, philosophical and cultural reasons,
none of the traditional apologetic systems has received the en-
dorsement of a substantial majority of Christian apologists. While
some recent Catholic apologists such as Maurice Blondel and
Pierre Teilhard de Chardin have embraced a uniquely Catholic
form of presuppositionalism, and some contemporary Calvinists
such as R. C. Sproul have embraced a form of evidentialism, the
incidence of presuppositionalism tracks closely the incidence of
theologians preferring a Calvinistic theology. Since evangelicalism has had decidedly Calvinist leanings in the last fifty years, it
is also probably safe to say that presuppositionalism has enjoyed a
majority within evangelicalism. But as evangelicalism becomes
more theologically diverse, the dominance of presuppositionalism

shows clear signs of moderating. Evidentialist apologetics reached the pinnacle of its influence in the nineteenth century but has waned substantially since then. Karl Barth's critique of apologetics hit evidentialism the hardest, with conservative Christians composing the lion's share of its remaining proponents. Recently, however, evidentialism has shown signs of a resurgence, perhaps as a counterbalance to the excesses of postmodernity. And experiential apologetics has also been on a roller coaster ride, having been embraced as the only real apologetic option by classical liberals in the late nineteenth and early twentieth centuries, seeing its influence wane somewhat due to the Barthian critique in the middle of the twentieth century, but recently enjoying a resurgence in certain circles of Western Christianity on the wings of postmodernity.

> *None of the traditional apologetic systems has received the endorsement of a substantial majority of Christian apologists.*

From the 1960s to the 1980s the debate between evidentialists and presuppositionalists raged throughout the halls of evangelical colleges and seminaries. While the debate is less shrill today than it has been, it is still worthwhile to briefly consider the sorts of arguments for and against the three traditional apologetics systems. I will, however, ignore what might be called intercategory debates—for example, the vigorous debates between historical apologists and classical apologists and between revelational and rational presuppositionalists.

An evaluation of the evidentialist strategy. In the past, some evidentialist apologists have held that the arguments for Christian belief were sufficient to produce certain beliefs that the central teachings of Christianity were true. Theistic arguments were, some held, proofs whose conclusions followed from self-evident or obviously true premises without any possibility of doubt or uncertainty. Today, however, such a position is extremely rare. Most evidentialists accept that arguments for God's existence are such that a sufficiently motivated skeptic can resist the intended conclusion. The typical goal of evidentialist apologetics is to argue that arguments and evidences are sufficient to demonstrate that belief in the Christian God is not only reasonable but more reasonable than other competing worldviews.

Nonevidentialists respond in a variety of ways. First, evidentialists have been charged with overestimating the scope of human reason. There are many beliefs that are widely held for which there is no persuasive argument—belief in other minds, the existence of the past and that we are not "plugged into" and controlled by a giant computer (as Neo was in the movie *The Matrix*). Second, many argue that evidentialists underestimate the deleterious effects of human sin. Sin affects not just our moral beliefs but also our reasoning and especially our willingness to submit to God's authority. Moreover, nonevidentialists are quick to point out that even if God reveals himself to his creation, it is far from obvious that God's existence would be equally obvious to all, regardless of their presuppositions or motives for seeking God. God might after all only grant knowledge of himself to those who seek with a subservient attitude. Third, nonevidentialists argue that evidentialists tend to oversimplify important theological matters, sometimes compromising theological integrity in order to state the evidence in its most persuasive manner. And there is always the risk that the desire to present the strongest possible evidential case for Christianity will lead those who embrace an evidentialist approach to treat evidence in a piecemeal fashion and ignore counterevidence. Finally, nonevidentialists argue that there is a fundamental disconnect between the best possible results of a theistic argument and the goal of biblical faith. Suppose a theistic argument demonstrated that the probability of Christian belief was 90 percent likely. This argument would place the believer in a situation analogous to the person who hears the weathercaster announce, "There is a 90 percent chance of rain this afternoon." In such a case, one might act as if it will rain (i.e., bring an umbrella), but one should not believe "It will rain." And if you did, your belief would be unjustified. Rather, one should believe "It is very likely it will rain."[17] And nonevidentialists object that the strength of this conclusion—"It is very likely that God exists"—is insufficient for grounding the level of commitment that accompanies biblical faith.

An evaluation of the presuppositional strategy. Presuppositional apologetics rightly places significant emphasis on the extent to which sin affects how humans view God, his revelation and our responsibility with respect to God's revelation. The differences between the Christian and the non-Christian do not merely amount to differences of opinion, but they are fundamentally different perspectives on reality. Moreover, Scripture makes clear that unbelievers do not just reject knowledge of God, they suppress knowledge of God. In a very real sense, their presuppositions blind non-Christians to the truth of Christian belief. Moreover, presuppositionalists join experiential apologists in arguing that mental assent to evidences for Christianity falls far short of the sort of commitment described in the Bible as faith.

The most fundamental objection to presuppositionalism is that presuppositionalists overstate their case in a variety of respects. Some forms of presuppositionalism, especially the revelational presuppositionalism of Van Til, significantly overstate the deleterious effects of sin on the reasoning of unregenerate humans. It is far from obvious that the unbelievers' failure to presuppose God's existence, authority and revelation makes it impossible for them to understand truths about the physical world and even about important aspects of the spiritual world. True, unbelievers cannot fully understand everything, but they might partially understand some things. Moreover, even if arguments and reasons are insufficient to produce biblical faith, that doesn't imply that they are irrelevant. And even if it might be theologically problematic to build a comprehensive apologetic approach solely from presuppositions already embraced by the unbeliever, that doesn't imply that an apologist cannot make effective use of arguments and evidences that appeal to presuppositions shared by Christians and non-Christians. Granted, it may be very difficult to find such common ground between the Christian and non-Christian. And even if it is found, the arguments will fall far short of fully proving Christianity. But if such arguments can increase the plausibility of Christian belief for a person or decrease his or her resistance to Christian belief, then it is difficult to see why they cannot be part of an apologist's arsenal.

An evaluation of the experientialist strategy. Experientialist apologetics rightly places emphasis on the necessity of experience. The Christian faith is not an abstract set of concepts to be believed but a life to be embraced, a life that includes all of a person—head, heart and hands, reason, emotion, and will. The Christian idea of salvation involves a transformative relationship with the creator of the universe. It is not merely about one's beliefs, for "even the demons believe" (Jas 2:19). Further, when asked, it is doubtful that a majority of mature Christians will say that their belief is based on argument. Rather, it is likely that their faith is based on the fact that they have experienced the risen Christ in prayer, in the liturgies and sacraments of the church, and in Christian community.

> The Christian idea of salvation involves a transformative relationship with the creator of the universe.

While many apologists make use of arguments based on religious experiences, experiential apologists are unique in their argument that experiential factors alone are sufficient to ground belief in God's existence. Evidentialists will push for rational explanations that support religious experiences, and presuppositionalists will object that human sinfulness affects not only our reasoning but also the interpretations of our experiences.

Those who build their apologetic approach solely on experiential factors have to overcome at least two hurdles: (1) alternative explanations of religious experience and (2) the diversity of religious experiences. While it may seem obvious to those having the experience that they have sensed God's presence, many other interpretations are possible, ranging from the skeptical to the arcane. Some may convince themselves that they have experienced God in order to help themselves deal with the difficulties of this world (Sigmund Freud) or in order to justify economic oppression (Karl Marx) or in order to lend credence to their aspirations and desires for power (Michel Foucault). Or a person might be deceived by a malevolent demon or hallucinating. Of course, none of this suggests that religious experiences cannot be genuine, only that it is possible that they are not.

A second objection to experiential approaches to apologetics comes from the diversity of religious experiences. While the lack of religious experience is not evidence against the possibility of genuine religious experiences (since absence of evidence is not evidence of absence), the presence of conflicting religious experiences does constitute a problem for experiential apologetics. While many people in many different cultures claim to have experienced God (in some sense), their experiences range widely. The experiential apologist must explain why the experiences of God that conflict with Christianity are not valid. An inability to do so is suggestive either that no religious experience is valid or that all are. In the former case, experiential apologetics is pointless; in the latter case, it would be difficult to call the experiences Christian.

The possibility of an eclectic apologetic methodology. In the past it was often assumed that the dividing lines between apologetic systems were clear and precise. Increasingly, however, it is acknowledged that there are no such clear lines. These three strategies that I have described are probably best described as ideal types—categories that are rarely perfectly exemplified. As conceptual tools, they have substantial value, but when they are applied to individual apologists, the lines that divide systems become profoundly blurred. This is because sometimes the differences between apologists represent fundamental philosophical and theological convictions and, as such, concern how apologetics must be practiced. Other times the differences between apologists in competing systems are merely pragmatic in nature, reflecting personally preferred styles of argumentation.[18] As such, they concern only how apologetics might be practiced.

To help account for the gray areas between apologetic strategies, we need a distinction. An apologist who is, for example, a presuppositionalist for fundamental theological or philosophical reasons, is a strict presuppositionalist, and one who embraces presuppositionalism for pragmatic reasons is an eclectic presuppositionalist. Strict presuppositionalists will reject the evidentialist and experientialist approaches as viable options. They will hold that there are theological or philosophical factors that make presuppositionalism the only viable approach. The same would go for strict evidentialists or strict experientialists. Cornelius Van Til is undoubtedly a strict presuppositionalist, Francis Schaeffer is not; John Locke is a strict evidentialist, Richard Swinburne is not; and Søren Kierkegaard is a strict experientialist, C. S. Lewis is not. While *eclectic apologists* might (and very likely will) prefer one approach over the others, they will not see their approach as the only viable one. Of course, an eclectic apologist might see one of the other approaches as severely problematic. For example, an eclectic evidentialist apologist might embrace aspects of experiential apologetics but absolutely reject presuppositionalism. And it is possible that an apologist will embrace aspects of all three methodologies.

Therefore, much as one can produce sixteen million different colors just from blending the three primary colors, one can employ a chromatic metaphor to explain the dizzying diversity of approaches to apologetics in terms of the emphasis each places on these three fundamental intuitions. Just as one can produce the color magenta by 255 parts blue, 255 parts red and 0 parts green, one might describe a particular apologetic approach as 100 parts evidentialist, 200 parts presuppositionalist and 50 parts experientialist. Some might see the rise of eclectic apologetic methodologies as symptomatic of postmodernism. The problem with this perspective is that long before our postmodern age, Augustine, Anselm and Pascal made use of an eclectic approach. And there are many contemporary apologists whose approach is best labeled eclectic. I will close this chapter by briefly mentioning just three.

There are many contemporary apologists whose approach is best labeled eclectic.

First, *Edward Carnell* (1919-1967) was a presuppositionalist who defended a substantial role for theological arguments and evidences. He held that "because we know God's existence and nature in our heart, we recognize Him in his handiwork."[19] But he also sought to "build on useful points of contact between the gospel and culture."[20] These points of contact included the law of noncontradiction, values, judicial sentiment and love. Part of the uniqueness of his apologetic approach is that he allowed it to be governed by specific situations. He said: "There is no 'official' or 'normative' approach to apologetics. . . . The approach is governed by the climate of the times. This means, as it were, that an apologist must play it by ear."[21]

Second, *C. Stephen Evans* models an eclectic approach to apologetics in his book *Why Believe? Reason and Mystery as Pointers to*

God. Strongly influenced by the emphasis on personal experience and mystery found in Søren Kierkegaard, he also finds a substantial role for theistic arguments. Experience and rational argument are not opposed to each other for Evans because while human beings are certainly rational beings, rational arguments can only take one so far. Drawing upon an insight developed by both Kierkegaard and Pascal, Evans asserts that while logical arguments may convince the mind, they make little impression upon the heart. Consequently, arguments based both on our observations of the world and on experiences of the mysterious can point us to God, says Evans. The case for Christianity will be based not on a single argument but on the sum total of evidence available from each and every aspect of human experience.

Finally, *Alvin Plantinga* blends aspects of presuppositionalism with experientialism. Ironically, Plantinga uses highly sophisticated philosophical arguments to demonstrate that religious belief need not, and even should not, be based solely on arguments. Further, following John Calvin, Plantinga argues that God has created humans with an innate experiential tendency—called the *sensus divinitatis*—to form beliefs about God in certain circumstances. For example, when viewing a starry sky, the *sensus divinitatis* might produce the belief "only God could have created all of this." While sin suppresses this innate ability, God's act of redemption can restore a degree of functionality of the *sensus divinitatis*. Plantinga, therefore, is opposed to evidentialism, but he is not opposed to giving arguments for God's existence. In fact, he has developed what some feel is a successful version of the ontological argument. And while he emphasizes the essential role of Christian experiences in his work, he does not do so in a way that excludes rational thought and argument. Finally, while Plantinga believes that the essential truths of the faith cannot be proved and therefore may be, in some sense of the word, presupposed by the Christian, nothing in his work suggests that Christians cannot or should not develop arguments to support their faith. He claims only that Christians need not do so in order to be rational.

KEY TERMS

meta-apologetic questions
relationship between faith and reason
rationalism
fideism
natural theology
Reformed theology
synergism
correspondence theory of truth
knowledge
Bernard Ramm
Gordon Lewis
evidentialist strategy
evidentialism
classical apologetics
historical apologetics
cumulative-case apologetics
presuppositionalist strategy
revelational presuppositionalism
rational presuppositionalism
practical presuppositionalism
experientialist strategy
one-step approach
two-step approach
many-step approach
no-step approach
eclectic apologetics
Edward Carnell
C. Stephen Evans
Alvin Plantinga

5

PHILOSOPHICAL OBJECTIONS
TO APOLOGETICS

Despite its prominent place in Christian history, apologetics currently has a bad reputation in many segments of contemporary Western culture. Stop an average person on the street and ask if she has a positive or negative picture of a Christian apologist. Assuming that she knew what the word *apologist* meant, she would likely register a negative opinion. Our culture is not enthusiastic about people who believe that their religious beliefs are true and that the beliefs of those who disagree with them are false. For this and other reasons, practically without exception, Christian apologetics has vanished from theology programs at state universities and mainline Protestant undergraduate and seminary programs. For example, the last time apologetics was offered at Princeton Theological Seminary, Franklin Roosevelt was still president of the United States.[1] And the Roman Catholic tradition of apologetics was dealt a substantial blow by the Second Vatican Council (1962-1965), which reduced it to a subdiscipline within the field of fundamental theology.[2]

Some of the objections to apologetics are in fact objections to particular varieties of apologetics. Karl Barth's diatribes against apologetics are, in large part, directed at revisionist apologists, like Schleiermacher, who are willing to dispense with aspects of orthodox Christian belief in order to get a "fair hearing" for Christianity by non-Christians. Moreover, Barth's rejection of the idea that general revelation was capable of providing knowledge of God places him at odds with most strands of evidentialist apologetics. But it is not at all obvious that he would quarrel with certain kinds of presuppositional apologists. And Barth certainly would have embraced an understanding of apologetics that involved the careful conceptualization and formulation of theological issues in a way that was both persuasive and preemptively handled the sorts of questions Christians, seekers and non-Christians ask. In fact, it is very plausible to see his massive *Church Dogmatics* as exactly that kind of apologetic work.

> Some of the objections to apologetics are in fact objections to particular varieties of apologetics.

Moreover, nearly everybody will object to the style of apologetics that has been all too common in Christianity. It is profoundly sad and undeniably true that many apologists have practiced apologetics in a way that has been intellectually sloppy, culturally insensitive, belligerent, condescending and arrogant. Let's call this sort of objection to apologetics an *as-practiced objection*. The problem here is not that people are engaged in defending the faith, but that they are doing it in a manner that is not remotely Christlike. Therefore, it is important to see that this entirely understandable objection to bad apologetics is not an objection to apologetics per se. (The matter of how to do apologetics appropriately and effectively will be the topic of the last chapter.)

But some of the objections to apologetics are what I will call *in-

principle objections. These objections amount to the claim that apologetics is, by its very nature, conceptually problematic and/or morally objectionable and, therefore, that it should cease as a Christian activity. In principle, objections are found in the mouths of atheists and committed Christians alike, although atheists typically appeal to different objections than Christians. In this chapter, I will discuss six different philosophical objections to apologetics, the sorts of objections more commonly appealed to by atheists. In the next chapter, I will consider biblical and theological objections to apologetics, the sorts of objections typically appealed to by Christians. Of course, these chapters do not address every possible in-principle objection to apologetics, only those that are most common. I will argue that none of these objections are successful. While some identify reasons to reject a particular approach to apologetics, none demonstrate the invalidity of apologetics per se.

I. THE OBJECTION FROM SKEPTICISM

Skepticism is the view that knowledge is impossible. A *global skeptic* holds that absolutely nothing can be known, even seemingly obvious beliefs like "I am sitting down right now" or "I see a book sitting on the table in front of me." A *local skeptic,* on the other hand, applies a skeptical attitude only to particular areas. One might be a skeptic about the existence of subatomic particles, holding that current technology is insufficient to give a meaningful account of such tiny objects. Some are local skeptics about moral principles. And I join all orthodox Christians in being a local skeptic about the possibility of *fully* comprehending God's nature. For our purposes, however, the most interesting form of local skepticism is religious skepticism.

The objection to apologetics from skepticism, therefore, comes in two forms: an objection from *global skepticism* and an objection from *religious skepticism.* The basic argument goes like this:

1. The task of apologetics is predicated on the idea that religious knowledge is possible.

2a. It is not possible to know anything at all (global skepticism).

2b. It is not possible to know anything about the religious realm (religious skepticism).

3. Therefore, apologetics is inappropriate.

Proposition (1) is true—engaging in apologetics assumes that there are truths about the religious world and that it is possible to have at least partial knowledge of those truths. And, if either (2a) or (2b) is true—if it is impossible to know anything about the religious world—then (3) follows. But is (2a) or (2b) true? In this section, I will discuss (2a), global skepticism; in the next I will discuss (2b), religious skepticism.

Global skepticism is built on the idea that any belief you hold could be false, even beliefs that seem undeniable. The global skeptic is famous for concocting elaborate, wildly implausible, but still logically possible scenarios in which even our most obvious beliefs are false. For example, if I am in the Matrix being fed visual stimuli by a computer program or if I am being systematically deceived by a malevolent demon, even apparently obvious beliefs like "I am sitting right now" will be false.

> *Global skepticism is built on the idea that any belief you hold could be false.*

One might respond to global skepticism by denying the possibility that one is in the Matrix or being deceived by a demon. It is difficult, however, to argue that such explanations, even if extremely unlikely, are impossible. A better approach is to point out that just because a belief of yours could be wrong doesn't mean that it is. After all, even if it is logically possible I am being deceived by a malevolent demon, it is also logically possible that I am forming beliefs with the assistance of a benevolent angel, who wants every belief I hold to be true. In fact, it is plausible to see the malevolent demon and the benevolent angel scenarios as being equally likely. In the face of these logically contradictory but equally possible scenarios, what should I do? I should realize that it is vastly more probable than either scenario that my situation is generally as it appears to be and that my beliefs are not being manipulated by an external agent, for good or for ill. This insight has been nicely expressed by Richard Swinburne. He argues for what he calls "the principle of credulity"—namely, the idea that in the absence of special considerations, if it seems to a subject that X is present, then probably X is present; what one seems to perceive is probably so.[3]

Consequently, acknowledging that even apparently obvious beliefs might be wrong does nothing to undermine the possibility of knowledge. Therefore, the objection to apologetics from global skepticism runs aground on the fact that it is more reasonable to be skeptical about the scenarios described by the global skeptics than about everyday beliefs like "I am sitting." An apologist can acknowledge that it is logically possible he could be wrong about his everyday beliefs and still confidently assert that what he believes is true and that knowledge is possible.

2. THE OBJECTION FROM RELIGIOUS SKEPTICISM

How about the objection to apologetics from religious skepticism? Religious skeptics typically accept the deliverances of their senses, the findings of science and the results of logical reasoning. They hold, however, that knowledge of the supernatural or religious realm is impossible. The trick for the religious skeptic is to come up with a logically consistent explanation of why nonreligious knowledge is possible and religious knowledge is not.

Some religious skeptics seek to define the concept of knowledge in such a way as to render knowledge of the supernatural realm impossible by definition. One such attempt involves arguing, first, that one can only have knowledge of things that can be perceived with the five senses and, second, that religious knowledge cannot be based on the senses. Another attempt to define religious language out of existence would involve claiming that only beliefs that are the result of the scientific method can be considered knowledge and, on this basis, arguing that religious knowledge could never come from the scientific method. However, these attempts to establish religious skepticism suffer from a common, crippling deficiency. They are both self-referentially incoherent. They assert a requirement for knowledge that they cannot meet themselves. The principle that knowledge must come from the senses does not itself come from the senses and, therefore, by its own lights, cannot be known. And if it cannot be known to be true itself, it is hardly sufficient to call into question the possibility of religious knowledge. Similarly, the principle that beliefs must be the result of the scientific method is not itself the result of the scientific method and therefore, if true, cannot be known.

Other religious skeptics take a different approach. Despairing of the attempt to define religious knowledge out of existence and building on the common-sense notion that poorly supported beliefs should not be considered knowledge, some religious skeptics argue that only beliefs that are based on sufficient evidence can be considered knowledge and then argue that the evidence for religious beliefs is insufficient. Of course, this sort of argument depends greatly on what is accepted as evidence and on what sufficient evidence looks like. Why think that evidence for religious belief is insufficient and that, therefore, apologetics is inappropriate? There are two typical answers to this question. The problem with religious evidence, we are told, is first that it is not "publicly accessible" and, second, that other religious traditions make competing claims to knowledge based on religious experience. In other words, religious beliefs are problematic in a way that everyday beliefs such as "I see a tree" are not. We cannot verify and check religious experiences in the way we can verify the presence of trees.

Notice that this objection assumes a pair of principles—knowledge must be public and knowledge of X is incompatible with disagreement about X—both of which are highly questionable. If religious skeptics object to religious knowledge on the grounds that it is not publicly accessible, they will also call into question the acceptability of beliefs about one's internal states such as "my knee hurts" or memory beliefs such as "I had toast and eggs for breakfast this morning," neither of which is publicly accessible in the relevant sense.[4] Pretty clearly, the requirement that knowledge must be publicly accessible is too strong. The principle that knowledge is incompatible with disagreement is similarly flawed. Such a principle would undercut knowledge that the Holocaust occurred, that the earth is not flat and that racism is immoral (for there are people that disagree with each of these things). Should we, in the face of the arguments of white supremacists, retract our claim that devaluing people because of their skin color is a moral abomination? Clearly not. The same applies to religious beliefs—the fact that some reject Christian beliefs does not entail that Christian beliefs are false or that Christians cannot be justified in believing as they do. Of course, the fact that skeptics or people of other religious traditions—people that may be both very sincere and highly intelligent—disagree with you is not irrelevant. We should take their beliefs as an opportunity to test our own beliefs. The point is that disagreement does not, by itself, eliminate the possibility of knowledge.

A default assumption of religious skepticism looks to be on shaky ground. Of course, in the final analysis, any particular claim to religious knowledge might turn out to be false. David Koresh (the leader of the Branch Davidian cult) and many others have claimed to hear directly from God. I am skeptical about their claims, but not about the possibility that somebody might hear from God. What is required is discernment. So in the final analysis, the possibility of religious skepticism does not undercut the validity of apologetics; it shows why it is necessary. Christians must do the difficult work of showing why Christian beliefs are different from the teachings of David Koresh. That is what apologetics is all about: discussing, defending and commending the good news about Jesus Christ.

3. THE OBJECTION FROM RELIGIOUS RELATIVISM

Relativism is the idea that beliefs are only true relative to a particular frame of reference or perspective. Your beliefs are only true for you or for your community or for your culture. There are, on this view, no universal truths. Global relativism—the claim that all beliefs are relative—is patently false, for if all truths are relative, so is the truth of the statement "All truths are relative." But this does not remove relativism as an option, for just as with skepticism, it is possible to be a local relativist; that is, it is possible to be a relativist about some things, but not others. In fact, everybody is (and should be) relativistic about some things.

> Relativism is the idea that beliefs are only true relative to a particular frame of reference or perspective.

Consider three different kinds of beliefs: (1) "The best-tasting pop is Dr Pepper," (2) "You should drive on the right side of the road," and (3) "A statement ('I am sitting') and its negation ('I am not sitting') cannot both be true at the same time and in the same sense." (The last of these is a law of logic called the law of noncontradiction.) The first of these statements is decided by personal preference, and the second is decided by community law. Consequently, one might say that there is no single right answer to the questions "What is the best-tasting pop?" and "On which side of the road should the law require people to drive?" These beliefs are decided, in the first case, by persons and, in the second case, by communities. They are not determined by reality. And they might be decided to be other than they are. Some people (for some reason unbeknownst to me) prefer Diet Pepsi to Dr Pepper, and some communities require drivers to drive on the left side of the road. The third belief, however, is not decided by anyone. It is part of reality, and all attempts to think and communicate assume this basic logical principle. I join the vast majority of people in being a relativist with respect to the best-tasting pop and the best side of the road to drive on, but not with respect to fundamental logical laws like the law of noncontradiction.

Religious relativism amounts to the claim that all religious beliefs are decided either by individuals or communities. In other words, religious beliefs reflect the values and commitments of people or communities; they do not describe reality. Consequently, according to religious relativists, religious beliefs like "Jesus is the Son of God" are more akin to "Dr Pepper is the best-tasting pop" than universally true beliefs such as the law of noncontradiction. Of course, religious relativists hold that religious beliefs are personally important, life-guiding, held with passion and might be considered true in some sense, but they are not universally or objectively true. The objection to Christian apologetics from religious relativism, therefore, amounts to the claim that the practice of Christian apologetics involves the attempt to universalize a category of beliefs that is not universal by nature. It would be like the CEO of Dr Pepper attempting to argue that you should buy Dr Pepper because it *really* is the best-tasting pop. Such an argument would (and should) be met with incredulity. Because there are no transpersonal or transcultural factors that determine what pop tastes the best, it seems utterly inappropriate to argue that a person who preferred Diet Pepsi to Dr Pepper was simply misguided and should change his or her preference. Similarly, if one's religious beliefs are nothing more than personal or cultural preferences, the attempt to defend and argue for one set of preferences over another is inappropriate. Religious relativism is increasingly popular in our culture and, if true, constitutes a profound objection to apologetics.

Before seeking to answer this question and defuse its objection to apologetics, another question is worth asking. Why would anybody want to believe religious relativism? Why think that there is no right answer to religious questions? The answer comes from what some people believe is the defining characteristic of our age—pluralism. The simple fact is that there are many different, mutually exclusive answers given to religious questions. The impetus toward religious relativism comes from the desire for harmony amongst our disagreements. Suppose I believe "Jesus is the Son of God" and my friend believes "there is one God Allah and Muhammad is his prophet." If religious relativism is true, then in a very real sense, both of our religious beliefs are true. And of course, since we are both right, engaging my friend in apologetic dialogue seems every bit as pointless as attempting to argue that Dr Pepper really tastes best. But such harmony demands a price. While in one sense religious relativism entails that we are both right, in another more substantial sense, both are wrong. In other words, according to the religious relativist, while religious beliefs are true in the sense that they accurately reflect your commitments, preferences and interpretations, they are false in the sense of describing the way reality is.

In order to respond to the objection to Christian apologetics from relativism, it is first essential to see that there is a healthy dose of nonsense in the way the relativist uses terms like *reality, truth* and *interpretation*. The relativist claims that each person creates his or her own reality and that truth is just one person's interpretation. This leads to such silliness as "Racism is wrong only if you say it is." A more sensible usage of these important terms is as follows: reality is what is, our beliefs about reality are our interpretations, and our interpretations are true to the degree that they accurately represent reality. There is, of

> *The idea of accurately representing reality is more complicated than it might seem on the surface.*

course, much more that could be said about these concepts, but let me offer just one refinement. The idea of accurately representing reality is more complicated than it might seem on the surface. While truth always is determined by its correspondence to reality, what constitutes correspondence between a belief and a fact is not as obvious as it might seem on the surface.

Consider the following three statements:

(1) "I have four kids."

(2) "There are fifty peaks over 14,000 feet in Colorado."[5]

(3) "I am five feet eleven inches tall."

The truth value of the first statement is a function not only of the number of children the author of the statement has but also of the intended meaning of the author. In my mouth, the first statement is true if I'm talking about children and false if I'm talking about baby goats.

The second statement shows how the social-linguistic context affects the truth value of statements. What seems to be a straightforward descriptive sentence is significantly complicated when one considers the definition of "a peak." How much drop in elevation is necessary before two adjacent points of higher elevation are considered different peaks rather than parts of the same peak?

Consequently, the truth value of the second statement depends on a socially constructed definition of what a peak is.

The truth value of the third statement depends not only on a person's actual height but on what degree of approximation is considered socially appropriate. Suppose when asked "How tall are you?" I answer: "five feet eleven inches." Does the statement "I am five feet eleven inches" correspond to reality? In one sense, no. I am, as it turns out, a bit under five feet eleven inches. But it would be weird (admittedly, not a technical term) if I said that I was five feet and 10.987654321 inches. (Of course, even that figure would be an approximation, albeit a much more precise one.) However, such approximation is a necessary part of communication and is governed by socially constructed norms. One might say that five feet eleven inches corresponds to reality as a socially appropriate approximation of my height. Rounding one's height up to the nearest foot, one's golf score down to the nearest ten and one's weight down to the nearest one hundred are probably not socially appropriate approximations—more's the pity. This is not to say that reality itself is socially defined or constructed, only that the descriptive terms we use to describe reality are a product of our social and linguistic contexts. Let's call this perspective *soft contextualism.*

Religious relativism embraces a more radical position, one that views one's religious beliefs as being determined by one's linguistic, social and cultural contexts. It's not just that our descriptive labels are linguistically or socially constructed; it's that reality itself is constructed, and therefore reference to reality is impossible. Let's call this position *hard contextualism.*

Religious relativism (and the hard contextualism that undergirds it) is deeply flawed. While our descriptions of reality must be indexed to a particular set of definitions about the terms we use to describe it, that does not suggest that reality itself is linguistically constructed. Just as the descriptive adequacy of the statement "I'm hungry" must be indexed to a particular time and person (for me, that's right before lunch), the descriptive adequacy of statements concerning the peaks of Colorado must be indexed to a particular (even if arbitrary) account of what constitutes a peak (as well as an account of fifty, 14,000 feet and Colorado). In other words, even if our interpretive and definitional frameworks play a role in how the world appears, it is still the world that appears to us, not some reality-divorced realm of mere appearances.[6]

Further, religious relativism is inconsistent. Religious relativists intend to impose on others the view that religious beliefs are not based on reality; rather they are a matter of personal and cultural preference. But this view itself is a religious belief based on a particular interpretation of religious reality (i.e., there is no religious reality or religious reality is not knowable or something similar) and therefore, by its own lights, not universally true. Christian apologetics, therefore, is no more inappropriate than the religious relativists' defense and articulation of their relativistic perspective on religious reality. As soon as religious relativists articulate their objection to Christian apologetics, they are doing the exact thing that the Christian apologist supposedly should not be doing.

4. THE OBJECTION FROM POSTMODERNISM

Few concepts are more hotly debated than postmodernism, and even when a definition is agreed upon, there is rarely agreement on whether postmodernism, thus defined, is a good or bad thing. Contrary to what some say, postmodernism is not the same thing as relativism. Some who embrace the label postmodern are relativistic, but there are also many who are not. The defining characteristic of *postmodernism* is best thought of as a loss of confidence in the modern project and its attempt to formulate perfect, indubitable answers to the questions humans ask. Postmodernism (in its nonrelativistic variety), therefore, does not question the possibility of truth or knowledge. It questions only whether our beliefs are absolutely certain and whether our descriptions of reality are perfect and exhaustive.

This loss of confidence in the modernistic quest for certainty was caused, at least partially, by the realization that all human knowledge is perspectival or contextual and, therefore, to some degree subjective. There is no perfectly neutral perspective from which we can assess the truth value of beliefs. We are always assessing things from our perspective and from within our context. The examples in the previous section regarding socially acceptable approximations show the impact of our perspective on our descriptions of reality. Our descriptive statements depend on socially defined uses of terms, and our descriptions are often approximations. In the previous section, we termed such a perspective soft contextualism. Of course, some who embrace the label postmodern want to take this much further; they desire to embrace hard contextualism. This more radical version of postmodernism is not only logically problematic; it is questionable given the intellectual humility supposedly entailed by postmodernism. Doesn't one have to possess a pretty complete and accurate picture of the relationship between human language and reality to claim that reality is wholly linguistically and socially constructed? Moreover, such a claim seems unjustified given the ability of different cultures and different linguistic systems to exchange information and communicate. Sure, communication is difficult and often not entirely clear, but it is possible—something that doesn't seem possible given the claim that reality is completely linguistically and socially constructed.

Setting aside the more radical version of postmodernism, is there anything in postmodernism that amounts to a valid objec-

> *Contrary to what some say, postmodernism is not the same thing as relativism.*

tion to apologetics? No. Acknowledging human limitations and the perspectival nature of human knowing does not undercut the task of defending and commending the faith. Knowledge is perspectival, not impossible; human knowledge is limited, not nonexistent. The claim that nonrelativistic postmodernism invalidates the task of apologetics makes no more sense than claiming that because our knowledge of physics is limited and fallible that any theory in physics is just as good as any other.

Of course, postmodernism undoubtedly constitutes an objection to certain forms of apologetics. The apologetic approach of a few strict evidentialists, for example, is incompatible even with nonrelativistic postmodernism. Postmodernism will rightly question the assumptions that facts are self-interpreting, certainty is possible, and arguments by themselves are sufficient to induce faith. In other words, postmodernism provides apologetics with an intellectual humility that has been sadly absent from too many apologetic endeavors in the past. Of course, the Christian shouldn't have needed the help from postmodernism here. Intellectual humility is something that should have always characterized Christian apologetics. In this sense, there is a convergence between the Christian acknowledgment that "now we see but a poor reflection as in a mirror" (1 Cor 13:12) and the postmodern acknowledgment of the effect of our perspectives, biases and assumptions on our knowledge. Consequently, nonrelativistic postmodernism is a friend to contemporary Christian apologetics in that it corrects some of the egregious blunders made by overly modernistic apologists in the past.

5. THE OBJECTION FROM THE IMMORALITY OF CHRISTIANITY
This objection to apologetics is inflammatory, but it is not at all uncommon. The essence of this objection is this: apologetics defends a belief system that has been responsible for oppression and violence. Sadly, this objection raises a point that is undeniable. Christianity has been used by some to justify slavery, deprive

women of even basic human rights and keep those in poverty from rejecting an oppressive status quo. Moreover, some individual Christians have leveraged their religious beliefs for financial gain, to gain political power, and to justify their abusive treatment of their children, parishioners or spouses. And Christian beliefs have been used, at times, as a means to keep people in a state of ignorance, reactionary legalism and spiritual deprivation. Not a pretty picture.

Nonetheless, this objection to apologetics suffers from the flaw of drawing a conclusion from part of the evidence. Two additional facts need to be considered. First, while it is undeniable that people who have claimed to be Christians have perpetrated great evil upon others, it is far from obvious that these people were being faithful to their Christian beliefs in doing so. I would argue, in fact, that these evil actions are decisively non-Christian. Second, this objection overlooks the fact that Christianity has been a tremendous force for good in the world. While Christians did attempt to justify slavery from Scripture, the abolitionist movements in both Great Britain and the United States were spearheaded by Christians who used biblical and theological arguments against slavery. Similar things might be said for the women's rights movement, the civil rights movement and other attempts to fight oppression in our world.

The crucial question, then, is whether the oppressions perpetrated by Christians are necessarily part of Christian belief and therefore unavoidable wherever Christian belief is found or whether they are abuses, misrepresentations and misapplications of Christian belief. If the former, then Christian apologetics should become extinct, but if the latter, then Christian apologetics is still viable, all the more so because the Christian apologist must join all other right-thinking Christians in condemning these bastardizations of Christian belief with the purpose of showing Christian belief for what it really is.

6. THE WHITE AND WESTERN OBJECTION

The final philosophical objection to apologetics is difficult to articulate precisely. The basic idea is that apologetics is tied to white and Western modes of thinking. The difficulty articulating this objection arises from the multiplicity of reasons that can be and have been offered for why it is a bad thing that apologetics is white and Western. For some, apologetics is problematic because it assumes patterns of theological belief, persuasion and logic that are either inappropriate or ineffective in non-white and non-Western contexts.[7] For others, the problem lies in the fact that apologetics is implicated in a long and tragic history of colonialization. For many years and in many contexts, the missionary apologist and the colonist were seen as identical, for with the Christian message came not only the dismissal and suppression of the indigenous culture, but also the subjugation of indigenous peoples. And while the active practice of colonialism has been sharply curtailed, today the presentation of the gospel in non-Western contexts continues to be tainted by the enduring impact of colonialism as well as by the affluence and political and economic policies of the West.

The objection that apologetics is white and Western is best seen as closely related to the previous two objections to apologetics. It draws on the relativism of hard contextualism in claiming that non-Western people approach theological reasoning and logical arguments in a way that is fundamentally incompatible with Western approaches. And it draws on the complaint that apologetics is inappropriate because Christianity has been a tool of oppression.

While this objection is definitely answerable, it must be acknowledged that Christians are to blame here, not just for our past history of oppression but for fueling the fires of hard contextualism. In the past, when Christian missionaries and apologists refused to acknowledge cultural differences and instead tried to import Western culture with their defense of the gospel message, they inadvertently reinforced the idea that Christianity and the task of Christian apologetics could flourish only in the context of white/Western culture. Consequently, an answer to this objection must include an acknowledgment that all theologies are contextual theologies. Western Christianity is not the cultural default to which every other culture must adapt to be truly Christian.

To answer this objection, first, Christians must acknowledge our past (and present) mistakes and seek to distance ourselves from them in word and deed. Only when we do so will we avoid the same (or similar) mistakes in the future. Second, it is crucial to confront the assumption that racial and cultural identities are the sole determinants of religious and moral beliefs. While the ethical and theological beliefs of the West are not true just because they are Western, neither are they false just because they are Western. Granted, in the past Western Christians have been guilty of dismissing non-Western values and beliefs. But the moral assessment of practices or beliefs enshrined in other cultures or races does not have to arise from racist or ethnocentrist sensibilities. As Charles Taylor says:

> When we stand with the moral outlook of universal and equal respect, we don't consider its condemnation of slavery, widow-burning, human sacrifice, and female circumcision only as expressions of our way of being, inviting a reciprocal and equally valid condemnation of our free labor, widow-remarriage, bloodless sacrifice, and sex equality from societies where these strange practices flourish.[8]

Finally, notice that the requirement that oppressors acknowledge their past mistakes assumes that it is possible for people of different races, cultures and classes to share a common truth and set of values—that oppression and exploitation are wrong. For if cultures could not share a common perspective, how could people in the oppressed culture recognize their oppressor's actions as unjustified and immoral and how could people in the oppressor's culture acknowledge their actions as hurtful and immoral?

None of this should be taken to suggest that crosscultural apologetics is easy. Cultural differences are substantial, and real effort must be put into the task of figuring out how non-Western cultures treat the evidences, arguments and appeals to religious experience. This does not mean denying the crosscultural value or applicability of logic; the law of noncontradiction is not only applicable in the West. But crosscultural apologists must acknowledge that their logical arguments will not have the same sort of effect in Nairobi, Mumbai or Bangkok as in Chicago. This does not, therefore, suggest that Christian apologetics is inappropriate outside the West; it means that Christians should be fully aware of the potential pitfalls and barriers to success. And as the numbers of Western Christians shrink in comparison to non-Western Christians, this task will become all the more important. In fact, crosscultural apologetics is probably the single most important task of apologetics for the twenty-first century.

KEY TERMS
as-practiced objections
in-principle objections
global skepticism
local skepticism
religious skepticism
religious relativism
postmodernism
soft contextualism
hard contextualism

6

BIBLICAL AND THEOLOGICAL
OBJECTIONS TO APOLOGETICS

Thus far, the objections to apologetics we have considered are typically found in the mouths of unbelievers. But there are a fair number of objections to apologetics that come from Christians. I will consider two categories of objections: those that (supposedly) come from Scripture and those that are based on theological reasoning. I will then close this chapter with a discussion of the value and importance of the task of apologetics.

I. BIBLICAL OBJECTIONS

There are two types of *biblical objections* to the task of apologetics. The first is more aggressive and involves the claim that there are specific and clear repudiations of the practice of apologetics in Scripture. The second objection is more modest. Rather than claiming that Scripture is opposed to the practice of apologetics, this objection claims only that the Bible does not address the topic of apologetics and therefore cannot be used to justify the practice of apologetics. The first objection, if true, entails that all those who accept the authority of Scripture must reject the practice of apologetics; the second, if true, means that Christian apologists must explain why it is important to engage in a practice that Scripture does not explicitly address or sanction.

There are specific repudiations of apologetics in the Bible. Those who object to the concept and practice of apologetics on biblical grounds will typically marshal a variety of passages that supposedly demonstrate the invalidity of Christian apologetics. I will consider three of the most commonly mentioned.

Luke 21:14-15. In Luke 21, Jesus predicts that his followers will be persecuted, and in Luke 21:14-15 he gives the following command to his disciples: "So make up your minds not to prepare beforehand to defend yourselves, for I will give you utterance and wisdom which none of your opponents will be able to resist or refute" (NASB). Since apologetics clearly involves studying and thinking about how objections might be answered, it is claimed that those who engage in apologetics disobey Jesus' command "not to prepare beforehand" and put themselves in a position to be unable to hear the words that Christ himself will give us.

> *It is claimed that those who engage in apologetics disobey Jesus' command "not to prepare beforehand."*

A number of responses to this objection are possible. First, since the context of the passage is clearly one of persecution and threat of imminent physical harm, it might be suggested that Jesus' command not to prepare beforehand applies only to such instances. The vast majority of occasions for apologetics, therefore, would constitute very different kinds of situations.

Second, the translation of the Greek word behind "prepare beforehand" is at issue. The New International Version translates the passage to instruct "not to worry beforehand how you will defend yourselves," suggesting not that you should not think about how to answer objections to the faith, but only that you shouldn't worry when you are called to do so. While this interpretation would constitute an effective response to the objection, it is not the best translation. The NIV translation seems to be a harmonization of this passage with other parallel passages in Matthew 10:19-20, Mark 13:11 and Luke 12:11-12, all of which are rightly translated "do not worry/be anxious."[1] In chapter 21, however, Luke uses a slightly different term (*promeletao*) from the one he uses in Luke 12 or from what is used in Matthew 10 or Mark 13. It is a technical Attic Greek term used to describe the practicing of a speech or oral presentation.[2] The best translation of *promeletao* in Luke 21, therefore, is not "do not prepare beforehand" but "do not rehearse" (NET). On this understanding, what Jesus commands his followers not to do is provide a canned, one-size-fits-all response—something that is very good apologetic advice!

Finally, if this passage is taken as claiming that thoughtful preparation undercuts God's provision of words in the moment, then that command amounts to a mandate of ignorance, for such a command would seem to apply to any kind of learning, including Scripture memorization, study of theology or biblical studies. Such a position is both unnecessary and unreasonable, however, for God's provision through his Spirit of the right words to say in a particular situation is not hindered by prior thought and study on the part of those through whom he speaks. In fact, one might make a very reasonable argument that the Spirit has more communicative options when speaking through a person who has studied and thought carefully about theological and apologetic matters.

1 Corinthians 2:4-5. In 1 Corinthians 2, Paul describes his approach to sharing the gospel with the Corinthians, and in 1 Corinthians 2:4-5, he says, "My message and my preaching were not with wise and persuasive words, but with a demonstration of the Spirit's power, so that your faith might not rest on men's wisdom, but on God's power." He says something quite similar a chapter earlier: "For Christ did not send me to baptize, but to preach the gospel—not with words of human wisdom, lest the cross of Christ be emptied of its power" (1 Cor 1:17). Anti-apologists argue that these passages amount to an indictment of apologetics since apologetics involves the usage of "wise and persuasive words." This is problematic, it is said, because such an approach relocates the authority of the gospel from the power of the spirit to the persuasiveness of human logic and teaching.

The error in this application of these passages comes from misunderstanding the specific, contextual meaning of Paul's reference to "wise and persuasive words" and "human wisdom" (which, translated literally, is rendered "wisdom of speech"). Paul is certainly not suggesting that unclear language, sloppy vocabulary and bad arguments are the best tools for sharing the gospel. In many places in the book of Acts, Paul is described as reasoning with and attempting to persuade (Greek: *dialegomai*) the men in the Jewish synagogues he visited (Acts 17:2, 7; 18:4, 19; 19:8-9; 20:7; 24:12, 25). The point of 1 Corinthians 2:4-5 is that Paul did not want to present the gospel in the language of a trained orator who applied very specific and formal rhetorical skills and devices in order to persuade his audience. Such rhetorical devices were common among both the Jewish rabbis and the Greek philosophers. He didn't want to merely win a battle of rhetoric and impress people with his argumentative skills. His goal was to present the gospel as clearly and powerfully as possible and allow the Holy Spirit to work in the hearts of his hearers. So there is nothing in these passages that suggests that using thoughtful, logical arguments in the service of defending and

> *Paul is certainly not suggesting that unclear language, sloppy vocabulary and bad arguments are the best tools for sharing the gospel.*

commending the faith is inappropriate.

Matthew 12:39-40. In Matthew 12:39 (and parallels in Mt 16:4; Mk 8:11-12; Lk 11:29), Jesus refused to give a sign or a proof of his authority to those who were questioning him. Similarly, some who object to the practice of apologetics argue that apologetics does exactly what Jesus refused to do—offer proofs or guarantees of truthfulness. They claim that we should neither offer nor demand arguments and reasons for the truthfulness of the gospel. We should simply believe.

Of course, Jesus did, on occasions, refuse to perform miracles for those who expected or demanded them. But this is not because Jesus was opposed in principle to giving reasons or doing things to support his authority. In Mark 2:10-11, for example, he says "But so that you may know that the Son of Man has authority on earth to forgive sins . . . I tell you, stand up, take your stretcher, and go home" (NET). And when John the Baptist's disciples asked Jesus if he was the Christ, Jesus offered his actions and teachings as proof of his calling and nature (Mt 11:2-6). His occasional unwillingness to give signs was a function of his awareness that some who sought reasons and signs were interested not in believing but only in seeing amazing events. But these events should be seen as exceptions, for most often Jesus carefully and thoughtfully answered questions, even when they were asked by those who were skeptical.

> *Jesus carefully and thoughtfully answered questions, even when they were asked by those who were skeptical.*

Apologetics is nowhere sanctioned in the Bible. In the face of the failure to demonstrate that there are Scripture passages that refute the practice of apologetics, some fall back on the claim that even if Scripture doesn't refute apologetics, it certainly doesn't sanction it. Those who press this point usually do so with a trio of arguments. The first is the *no-details argument*. Some of the detractors of apologetics argue that the Bible does not provide any specific instructions on how to do apologetics, suggesting that apologetics is unnecessary or perhaps even inappropriate. This argument is flawed in a couple of respects. First, it is simply not the case that Scripture says nothing about how to approach apologetic encounters. The Bible says quite a lot about how Christians should interact with others as we share and defend the gospel. We should defend the gospel with "gentleness and respect" (1 Pet 3:15) and "without being frightened in any way by those who oppose you" (Phil 1:28), to name just a pair of examples. Second, the fact that there is no formal system of apologetics that is taught in Scripture does not suggest that it is a task that should be rejected. There is no formal system of hermeneutics (the study of the interpretation of Scripture), homiletics (the study of preaching), ethics (the study of moral oughts) or even theology (the study of the essential concepts of Christianity), but that fact doesn't mean that any of these disciplines are unnecessary or inappropriate.

A second argument that the bible doesn't sanction apologetics is the *no-clear-examples argument*. Such an argument must contend with the obviously apologetic nature of Paul's argument on Mars Hill in Acts 17:16-34. Some dismiss this passage as a single example that clearly failed and was never repeated. We are to learn, it is said, from the mistake Paul made on Mars Hill. This perspective reflects a significant misunderstanding. The uniqueness of Paul's approach is a function of the uniqueness of the Mars Hill context. The vast majority of Paul's presentations of the gospel were in contexts where his audience knew the Old Testament and accepted its authority, unlike his audience on Mars Hill. Moreover, Mars Hill cannot reasonably be judged to be a failure. The recorded response to his words was that some scoffed, some wanted to hear more, and some believed (Acts 17:32-34). If this is failure, then every presentation of the gospel has been a failure.

But Acts 17:16-34 is not a solitary example. Another passage that clearly appears to sanction apologetics is 1 Peter 3:15, "But in your hearts set apart Christ as Lord. Always be prepared to give an answer to everyone who asks you to give the reason for the hope that you have. But do this with gentleness and respect." Those who object to the practice of apologetics respond that the immediate context of this passage is not intellectual objections to the faith, but persecution. Consequently, it is claimed that this passage is referring only to a situation unique to the early church, to the legal defense Christians were compelled to give when subjected to persecution at the hands of the Roman authorities. While this passage clearly refers at least to the response Christians were called to give when brought before the Roman authorities, the language used in the verse makes it impossible to restrict the application of this verse to a formal inquiry by the Roman government. The Greek word for "asks" (*aitein*) suggests an informal, spontaneous conversation, not merely a formal inquiry. And the generality of this language in this verse—"always be prepared" and "to anyone who asks"—makes it difficult to restrict the application of this verse only to those being persecuted. In fact, since all Christians in the first century were in imminent danger of persecution (from Jews or Romans), it is clear that Peter's apologetic mandate was intended as a standing order for all Christians.[3]

Others will press the no-clear-examples argument by claiming that the Bible assumes God's existence; it never argues for it. The problem with this argument is that, with the exception of a few schools of Greek philosophy, atheists were practically nonexistent in the ancient world. So while the Bible does not address the question often debated in our context—Does God exist?—there are many places where Scripture addresses a different, but equally important apologetic question: Which God exists? Therefore, it is not that the Bible doesn't employ apologetic arguments, but that the apologetic arguments found in the Bible are sometimes not recognized by us because our context is very different.

In fact, the Bible records many instances when powerful responses were given to questions about the authority of God's teachers or prophets. The creation account in Genesis is a clear refutation of other creation accounts of which ancient Israelites would have been aware, and the signs performed by Moses (Ex 4:1-9) and Elijah (1 Kings 18) supported their claim that Yahweh was real and that the gods of the Egyptians and Canaanites were not. Further, the Gospels themselves can be seen as apologetic in nature, for they include ample apologetic material for early Christians in their debates with Jews—that Jesus was descended from David, that he was born in Bethlehem and that he fulfills Old Testament messianic prophecies. Finally, Jesus himself responded clearly and cogently to a wide range of objections brought against him, his actions (Lk 6:1-11), his teachings (Jn 5:2-15) and the actions of his disciples (Mt 9:14). Sometimes his answer involves an action, as it did when he healed the paralyzed man as an answer to the objection that he did not have the authority to forgive sins (Mk 2:3-12). Other times his defense is either a direct response to a question (Mt 11:2-5; 12:22-29; Jn 5:19-47) or a demonstration that an objection itself is baseless or confused (Lk 20:1-8, 20-40; Jn 8:3-11).

The final argument that the bible does not sanction apologetics is the *no-need argument*. The Bible, it is claimed, does not need to be defended. Apologetics does nothing to add to the authority of the Bible. In one sense, this is true: apologetic arguments do not give Scripture its authority any more than our belief in God makes him exist. But apologetics is not about actual authority but about perceived authority. Apologetics is called for when people (either Christians or skeptics) have objections that prevent them from acknowledging the authority of Scripture. Perhaps God could have created the world in such a way that apologetics was not necessary. But in the world he has created, it seems clear that he has called Christians to partner with him in proclaiming, teaching and, where necessary, defending the good news of his son Jesus Christ.

2. THEOLOGICAL OBJECTIONS

Some of the people who object to apologetics admit that there are no philosophical objections to the practice and also admit that there are no specific passages that explicitly condemn apologetics. Nevertheless, they claim that the practice of apologetics is problematic in light of broad themes clearly taught in Scripture. I will consider six of the most common *theological objections*.

Human sinfulness. A very common objection to the practice of apologetics concerns the *sinfulness of human reason*. Sometimes called the noetic effects of sin (the word *noetic* comes from the Latin word for "mind": *nous*), the basic idea is that sin mars not only the human will and emotions, but also the intellect. The problem this supposedly poses for apologetics is that Christians and non-Christians are not really speaking the same language since the mind of the unbeliever is clouded by sin. First Corinthians 2:14 is commonly cited to support this contention: "The man without the Spirit does not accept the things that come from the spirit of God, for they are foolishness to him, and he cannot understand them, because they are spiritually discerned." In this view, apologetic arguments are problematic because they are presumptive; they involve humans trying to come to knowledge of God on their own terms rather than submitting to God's means of making his nature and plans known.

There is extensive and undeniable biblical data supporting the sinfulness of human beings, including the propensity toward sinfulness in human reasoning. We are inclined not only to sin but to cover up and justify our sin. The debate concerns the nature and extent of the effects of sin on the human mind. While the noetic effects of sin cannot be denied, neither should they be misunderstood. Unbelievers can still do math, logic and quantum physics. In fact, atheists such as A. J. Ayer, Bertrand Russell and Ayn Rand are, by any reasonable standard, geniuses. So it is not the case that non-Christians are unable to think. Neither is it the case that they are unable to understand the concepts of the gospel of Jesus Christ. Unbelievers understand the concepts of sacrifice, love and submission. The problem with unbelievers lies not in the functioning of their cognitive abilities but in their unwillingness to submit their lives to Christ.

The reasons behind this unwillingness to submit cannot be oversimplified. Invariably, people who reject Christ do so for many reasons. They may have been hurt by Christians, they might be angry at God, and undoubtedly, they dislike the idea of submitting their will to anybody, even God. Woven throughout their matrix of reasons for rejecting Christ, however, are beliefs that are contrary to Christianity and misunderstandings of the details and implications of scriptural teaching. And those beliefs and misunderstandings can and should be confronted and explained. Consequently, while apologetic arguments alone are insufficient to bring anyone to faith, they can break down intellectual barriers to the gospel and expose the intellectual bankruptcy and self-destructive nature of anti-Christian presuppositions.

God's transcendence. The second theological objection is similar to the first. But instead of the barrier to apologetics being found in human sinfulness, the barrier is located in God's utterly transcendent nature. It has always been part of orthodox Christianity to affirm that God is not merely quantitatively greater than his creation, but qualitatively different. Scripture describes God's judgments as "unsearchable" (Rom 11:33-34), and the impossibility of fully knowing God is one of the primary themes in the book of Job (Job 11:7-8; 37:5). While *God's transcendence* has always been a part of the Christian tradition, some theologians have taken these themes even further, holding that God is strictly unknowable and incomprehensible. God's infinity, trinity and simplicity, the fact that he does not have a body, and his "not being a being like other beings in this world" are all held up as reasons why humans cannot refer to God using finite human language or have any true beliefs about God's nature. And, of course, if humans are unable to say true things about God, the task of apologetics becomes extraneous at best.

A response to this objection to apologetics—which, note, is simultaneously an objection to all forms of theology—must not, as has too often been the case, downplay God's transcendence. God's nature is not like ours, and finite human minds cannot fully grasp or describe his being. Rather, our ability to refer to God, to speak about him and to say things that are true about his nature must be seen, like salvation, as a gift of God's grace. We can know God, despite his utterly transcendent nature, because he created us with the capacity to know him and because he has revealed himself to us—directly, in history and in speech, in writing, and through his Spirit. While Scripture is clear that humans cannot fully conceptualize God's nature, it assumes that we can know some things about God and holds humans accountable for false understandings of God. Our ability to know God, therefore, is not because God is intrinsically knowable, but because God has created us with such a capacity. Romans 1 talks about how God's attributes can be seen in what he has created. John Calvin talked about the *sensus divinitatis* that gives all people an awareness of God's character. And C. S. Lewis talked about a God-shaped hole in every human heart which produces a longing for God. Consequently, knowledge of God is possible—and, there-

> *Our ability to refer to God, to speak about him and to say things that are true about his nature must be seen, like salvation, as a gift of God's grace.*

fore, apologetics is possible—because we are the creation of a God that desires to be known by his creation.

Irrelevance of logical arguments to faith. A third theological objection to Christian apologetics emphasizes the *irrelevance of logical arguments* in the area of religious belief. This objection highlights the fact that there are many people that have (by all appearances) a robust, dynamic, sincere faith who have no arguments whatsoever for the propositions entailed by their faith: God exists, the Bible is trustworthy, etc. So logical arguments do not seem to be necessary for faith. But some push this line of thinking further; not only are logical arguments unnecessary for faith, but they are injurious to it. Albert Schweitzer lambasted what he called "the crooked and fragile thinking of Christian apologetics" that focused on intellectual arguments and ignored the inward, spiritual dimension.[4] The speculative, theoretical approach to Christian belief that accompanies apologetic arguments actually undercuts a vital, experiential relationship with God. And the logical arguments associated with apologetics, if they suggest the existence of a god of any sort, point not to the Christian God but to a vague, semi-deistic God of the philosophers who is relationally remote and unaffected by genuine religious concerns.[5] The conclusion to be drawn, given this line of thinking, is that apologetic arguments are at best misplaced and at worst dangerous as a means to faith.

There are two responses to this objection. First, while it is not problematic to admit that for any given person, logical reasons and arguments are unnecessary for faith, that does not suggest that logical reasons and arguments have no function in the Christian community. Suppose no Christian had ever found it possible or desirable to answer the problem of evil—the claim that the existence of evil suggests that an all-powerful, perfectly loving God cannot exist. Whenever that objection was made, Christians responded with nothing but silence. Even if Christians continued to

fight against evil in the name of Jesus Christ, after a while the reasonableness of fighting evil in Christ's name would be questioned.
Why not just fight evil? Why the unnecessary and unreasonable
appendage of a religious rationale for fighting evil? Consequently,
while it is absolutely true that rational arguments are not the cause
of Christian conviction, it does not follow that rational arguments
have no value. As Austin Farrer said, "For though argument does
not create conviction, the lack of it destroys belief. What seems to
be proved may not be embraced; but what no one shows the ability
to defend is quickly abandoned."[6] Similarly, while apologetic argument does not create belief, it creates an environment in which
belief can flourish. After all, no one would claim that the atmos-
phere is unnecessary because it does not create life. Similarly, it is
unreasonable to claim that apologetics is unnecessary (or worse)
because it does not, by itself, create faith.[7]

Second, while it is true that many of the rational arguments
for God's existence suggest only that God must be the cause of
all that exists, does this mean that Christian apologetics reduces
God to a vague, semi-deistic, God of the philosophers? It would
do so only if one relies solely on logical arguments and ignores
the broader picture of God presented in Scripture. But not only
would this be theologically problematic; it would be bad apologetics. Rational arguments have their function, but they only
provide part of the picture. To be faithful to Christianity, the
Christian apologist absolutely must rely on Scripture to provide
a complete picture of who God is. And any apologetic argument
that conflicts with the teachings of Scripture regarding God's
nature should be rejected.

Sola gratia. The fourth theological objection to Christian apologetics involves the claim that salvation comes to humans *sola
gratia,* or only through God's grace. Salvation cannot be achieved
by human effort, and since only the Holy Spirit can bring a person
to faith in Christ, it is unreasonable to engage in the sort of ac-

tivities suggested by apologetics. It is, of course, true that grace is necessary for salvation. Scripture is very clear that salvation is the work of the Holy Spirit (Eph 2:8-9; Tit 3:4-7). But if accepting that the Holy Spirit alone can bring a person to Christ entails that human activity is unnecessary, such a perspective would also invalidate witness, preaching, evangelism, teaching and any form of missionary outreach.[8] And that would clearly run counter to the Great Commission in Matthew 28:19: "Therefore go and make disciples of all nations, baptizing them in the name of the Father and the Son and the Holy Spirit" (NET). Moreover, the assumption that the work of the Holy Spirit makes apologetics unnecessary overlooks the fact that for some reason God has chosen to partner with humans in the process of spreading the gospel. Of course, that fact probably says more about his desire for us to learn from partnering with his Spirit than it does about his need for our involvement, but nevertheless it clearly seems that God has chosen to allow human beings a role in bringing the gospel to the world. Finally, there is nothing in Scripture that says or implies that the Holy Spirit works in the lives of people apart from evidence, reasons and arguments. In fact, the success of apologetic arguments depends crucially on the presence and action of the Holy Spirit. For this reason, it is far more reasonable to say that the Holy Spirit works through good arguments and reasons for the Christian faith rather than in spite of them or apart from them.

> *The success of apologetic arguments depends crucially on the presence and action of the Holy Spirit.*

Consequently, even if apologetic arguments are not directly the cause of faith, they can be very useful in helping both unbelievers and believers with questions. They can confirm and support belief reached in other ways, they can remove intellectual obstacles to confident commitment to Christ, and they may move fence sitters closer to Christian belief.[9] Most fundamentally, apologetic arguments can bring a person to a place where he or she can hear the leading of the Holy Spirit. In other words, the task of apologetics is to lead the horse to the water, but it is left in the hands of the Holy Spirit whether the horse will drink.

The cure is worse than the disease. The fifth theological objection to apologetics flows from concerns about the result of apologetics. On this view, while apologetics is an understandable attempt to deal with real and substantial objections, the *cure apologetics offers is worse than the disease,* and worse in two different ways. First, while the faith is simple and clear, apologetics makes the faith too complex, and, second, apologetics compromises essential truths of the faith and thereby destroys what it is trying to defend.

Those who articulate the first variety of this objection often appeal to passages like Mark 10:15. Speaking to his disciples, Jesus says: "I tell you the truth, whoever does not receive the Kingdom of God like a child will never enter it" (NET). Some have seen in this passage (and in the parallels in Mt 18:3 and Lk 18:17) a repudiation of apologetics. While childlike faith is simple and pure, the arguments formulated by apologists are complex and extremely difficult to understand. The problem with apologetics, therefore, is that it makes complex what should be simple and intellectualizes what should be approached with trust.

This objection is based on a pair of confusions. Perhaps the goal of some apologists has been to demonstrate their intellectual prowess by making the gospel of Jesus Christ appear as complex as possible, but that has not been the norm and it is certainly not necessary. Good apologetics is not about injecting complexity and confusion into the gospel in an attempt to make it sound more profound. Rather it is about communicating the profundity of the gospel in a manner that removes or mitigates actual or potential confusions. Moreover, there is a very important sense in which the faith is not simple. True, the gospel of Christ is clear and straightforward. But there are unavoidable and very complex questions that arise very quickly when thinking about the implications, scope and nature of the gospel. To the degree that apologetics deals with very complex issues, it does so because questions surrounding God's nature and existence, human nature, and God's action in the world raise some complex issues. And it is monumentally unhelpful to pretend that these issues are either not real or not really that complex. Consequently, the task of apologetics is to deal with the complex and difficult issues associated with the religious belief in such a way as to help people see the clarity and simplicity of God's offer of salvation for their lives.

The second variety of this objection—that apologetics compromises essential truths of the gospel—is a salutary warning. Unfortunately, there have been apologists in the past who have been willing to remove or modify aspects of the faith in order to broaden its appeal. In chapter three, this approach to apologetics was termed revisionist apologetics. Revisionist apologetics is absolutely unacceptable from the perspective of orthodox Christian belief. But notice that this objection is again only an objection to apologetics done badly. Karl Barth's famous objection to apologetics is an objection to "theological activity which, for the sake of getting to grips with unbelief, loosens or even loses its hold upon essential Christianity."[10] In building his objection, Barth sets up the following dilemma: either Christians adopt the perspective of the unbeliever or they do not. If they do not, they cannot take seriously the objections of the unbeliever; if they do, then they compromise the Christian faith. The problem with this objection is that when Barth describes apologetics, he describes a practice that very few if any apologists would actually embrace—one of going out to do apologetics while waving the white flag. In fact, when Barth makes these statements, he is explicitly reacting to the apologetics of Friedrich Schleiermacher.[11] And he is right to object to this kind of apologetic practice. Where he is wrong is in assuming that all forms of apologetics will, of necessity, fall into the same trap. Consequently, the dilemma Barth sets up for apologetics is a false dilemma. It is possible to take seriously the demands of non-Christians for rational arguments and evidence without compromising the faith. Of course, it must be acknowledged that the core beliefs of Christianity cannot be proved to the satisfaction of the skeptic and that Christian belief is based on a lot more than intellectual arguments. But neither of these acknowledgments undercuts the importance and value of arguments for the Christian faith.

So it is not necessarily the case that the cure (apologetics) is worse than the disease (unanswered objections to the faith). But the anti-apologist, at this point, might simply respond like this: Okay, it's possible that Christian apologetics might not be harmful, but given that it has been so harmful and given that it still might be in the future, isn't it prudent to avoid the entire practice? Two answers must be given. First, as a general principle, avoiding anything that could result in harm is not wise. Such a principle would seem to suggest that swimming, driving a car, childbirth, new relationships and eating are all practices that should be abstained from. Second, this sort of response tends to underestimate the virulence of the disease. The inability to answer substantial and legitimate questions about the faith will either cause a person to reject the faith or to remove faith from the realm of reason. And it's not obvious that in the long term the latter option is better than the former. Even if people who embrace what they take to be an irrational faith are able to maintain their commitment throughout their lives, how can they pass the faith on to the next generation? Why would their children or students accept such an understanding of the faith? Therefore, the fundamental flaw of removing the Christian faith from the sphere of rational belief is that it fails the generational test. Even if it works for this generation, it will likely be rejected by the next.

Social action is more important than doing apologetics. A final theological objection to Christian apologetics is that there are much more important things to do than answer the objections of skeptics. Jesus did not say that the unbelieving world would know him by the quality of arguments they gave; he said that believers would reveal him by the way they demonstrated Christlike love to their neighbors. The intensity of this objection is heightened by the sadly undeniable fact that all too often Christians have not adequately demonstrated Christ's love to those in need.

By way of response, it must be noted that addressing the social needs in the world and doing apologetics are in no way mutually exclusive. While it is obvious that the concerns of the Christian apologist are no substitute for other Christian responsibilities, that fact does not call into question the practice of Christian apologetics. From a Christian perspective, action and belief must be connected. As Gordon Lewis says: "By all means feed the starving, clothe the destitute, and offer a cup of cold water to the thirsty. But in whose name? And why in Christ's name and not another?"[12] Those who say that "it doesn't matter in whose name you act, as long as you act" are shortsighted. Action and belief are connected in all sorts of subtle ways. When one abandons or ignores the belief (or belief system) that motivates a particular course of action, who is to say that the action will continue in future generations? And even if it did, even if every social need was met as Christianity withered, wouldn't this be something like gaining the world but losing your soul? So while apologetics is no replacement for social action, neither is social action an adequate replacement for apologetics. Both are important, and the attempt to play one off

> *Addressing the social needs in the world and doing apologetics are in no way mutually exclusive.*

against the other is kind of like arguing whether it is more important to eat or breathe. Sure, breathing, like social action, might be the more pressing need, but over time if one does not eat, eventually one will also be unable to breathe.

3. THE VALUE AND IMPORTANCE OF APOLOGETICS

None of the philosophical, biblical or theological objections to apologetics are successful. Some suggest that particular approaches to apologetics are problematic, and many highlight the past mistakes of Christian apologists, but none suggest that the practice as a whole is invalid. In answering these objections, we have also seen some of the benefits of apologetics. I will close this chapter by making explicit the four most important reasons to do apologetics.

Apologetics is commanded by God. The first reason for apologetics is simple and straightforward. God commands that Christians "always be prepared to give an answer to everyone who asks you to give the reason for the hope that you have" (1 Pet 3:15). But this doesn't mean that Christians should wait until they are asked to defend their faith. In 2 Corinthians 10:5, Christians are also called to "demolish arguments and every pretension that sets itself up against the knowledge of God, and we take captive every thought to make it obedient to Christ." In Jude 3, the author urges believers who had been inundated with false teaching "to contend earnestly for the faith that was once for all entrusted to the saints" (NET). And finally, in Titus 1:9, Paul says that a leader of the church "must hold firmly to the trustworthy message as it has been taught, so that he can encourage others by sound doctrine and refute those that oppose it."

Does this mean that every Christian is required to be an apologist? Yes and no. All Christians are called to live their lives in ways that present the gospel of Jesus Christ in a compelling light. So one might say that all Christians are called to do *lifestyle apologetics.* But only some Christians will be called to the task of developing arguments for the Christian faith and being on the front line of the dialogue between Christianity and the exponents of other belief systems. This is a body-of-Christ issue. Some parts of Christ's body must take up the mantle of apologetics, but not all will take it up in the same sense. Moreover, as with the gift of teaching, Christians need to be wary of the call to Christian apologetics. Just as James 3:1 warns, "Not many of you should become teachers, my brothers and sisters, because you know that we will be judged more strictly" (NET), so also there is a real danger for those who practice Christian apologetics. The apologist's desire to answer questions is a good thing, but it is a very short distance from "I have an answer" to "I have all the answers." Intellectual arrogance is the Achilles' heel of the apologist, and the tendency toward it must be first acknowledged and then fought.

Apologetics is necessary in our culture. The second reason to do apologetics calls attention to our current context. Very few of the prevailing concepts in our culture are religiously neutral, and many of the most popular notions in our culture are poisonous to the essentials of the Christian faith. Notable examples include:

1. Real knowledge comes from the five senses.

2. Faith is "believing what you know ain't so" (Mark Twain).

3. Belief in God's existence is for the uneducated and weak-minded.

4. What we call miracles are just unique events that science has yet to explain.

5. Believing that your religious beliefs are true and those of others who disagree with you are false is inherently arrogant and intolerant.

6. Jesus Christ was a good moral teacher, but most of what is said about him in the Bible was made up by the church.

These ideas will not just go away if ignored. Like weeds in a garden, they need to be extracted and destroyed. But not only that. It would be shortsighted to envision the task of apologist merely as a weed puller. The ground also needs to be cultivated in a way that encourages authentic expressions of the Christian faith and interactions of Christianity with contemporary culture to flourish. The great American theologian J. Gresham Machen says this well:

> False ideas are the greatest obstacles to the reception of the gospel. We may preach with all the fervor of a reformer and yet succeed only in winning a straggler here and there, if we permit the whole collective thought of the nation or of the world to be controlled by ideas which, by the resistless force of logic, prevent Christianity from being regarded as anything more than a harmless delusion. Under such circumstances, what God desires us to do is to destroy the obstacle at its root.[13]

This is not to suggest that only those who are able to do apologetics, able to engage at a high level with the arguments that arise in our culture, really know their religious beliefs. I absolutely believe that my grandmother, who was no philosophically trained apologist, knew that Jesus Christ was her Savior, and that she knew this in a robust, authentic sense of that word. Any attempt to restrict knowledge only to those who can give technical arguments for how and why they believe what they do is wrong-headed. Likewise, my five-year-old daughter knows if there is a tree in front of her even if she cannot begin to articulate arguments for the reliability of sense perception or answer skeptical objections to her belief. So apologetics is not personally or epistemologically necessary; that is, it is not necessary for every person or necessary for knowledge. But it is, one might say, culturally necessary. Unless there are some who are willing to stand in the gap and confront the anti-Christian ideologies so prevalent in our culture, before long the faith my grandmother embraced will be seen as obsolete and will eventually become all but extinct.

Theological education requires an appropriate emphasis on apologetics. If we knew that this was the last generation and that Jesus was coming back in a few years, then the purpose of the detailed arguments associated with academic theology and apologetics would be of minimal value. But since we do not know when Jesus is coming back, the requirement to go and teach about the good news of Jesus Christ is firmly laid upon us. Unfortunately, the all-too-common suspicions about apologetics have created a crisis of theological education in many corners of the Western world. Former dean of Duke Divinity School Dennis Campbell says this brilliantly:

> [In our educational efforts] it is not that we have failed to be global, or that we have failed to take adequate account of the setting, or of the oppressed, but that we are not sure that religion is ultimately significant, that Christianity is true, and that the proclamation of the gospel is critically important for everyone everywhere.[14]

Without a conviction of the truthfulness of the Christian message and without some capacity to answer the questions that arise when teaching about the good news of Jesus Christ, theological education quickly loses both its *theos* and its *logos*. Theological education becomes less about God and more about humans, less about teaching and persuading and more about indoctrination. Teaching about the gospel involves not only doing apologetics, of course, but if one is unsure whether the gospel is anything more than a nice story, it is clearly impossible to teach the gospel in a way that is compelling and clear.

Meaningful dialogue requires a perspective that is supportive of apologetics. The final reason apologetics is a crucially important task for Christians might be initially surprising. Sadly, since some Christian apologists have been more interested in aggressive and demeaning monologues rather than respectful and open-minded dialogue, apologetics has been commonly seen as a barrier to dialogue. In fact, the mindset that animates apologetics is absolutely necessary to authentic dialogue. For authentic dialogue to occur between two parties with differing beliefs, each party must believe that (1) both are talking about the same issue and (2) the different perspectives are not merely a matter of personal preference. After all, how much dialogue can there really be between people who believe that my belief and my dialogue partner's belief, a belief which contradicts mine, are both true? By way of illustration, try to imagine an extended, thoughtful, mutually informative discussion on "Which color is the prettiest?" Moreover, if you believe that you and your dialogue partner have contradictory beliefs but do not talk about the fact that your beliefs are contradictory, if you ignore the reasons why you still hold your belief in the face of legitimate alternatives, have you really had a meaningful dialogue? A discourse that seeks only to understand a perspective but does not engage with the truth value, rationale and reasons offered for that perspective is, in the words of Paul Griffiths, "pallid, platitudinous, and degutted. Its products are intellectual pacifiers for the immature: pleasant to suck on but not very nourishing."[15] Meaningful dialogue is only possible between people who acknowledge both the importance of truth and the possibility that one (or both) perspectives represented in the conversation might fail to be true.

The fear of apologetics as a barrier to interreligious conversation is understandable. Religious beliefs are deeply personal and held with passion. Conversations that end up suggesting that one's religious commitments may be false are disconcerting. But the alternative is worse. John Stackhouse says this very well:

To abandon apologetics is to abandon the enterprise that animates religious people the world over: to find the truth and to live in its light the best we can. It is to abandon honest and searching dialogue that might result in someone actually changing his or her mind for the better, and to settle instead for mere understanding, or at least tolerance, of others' views while, indeed, remaining generally unmoved by them—since one has not taken them on as serious alternatives to one's own views.[16]

KEY TERMS

biblical objections to apologetics
theological objections to apologetics
no-details argument
no-clear-examples argument
no-need argument
human-sinfulness objection
God's transcendence objection
objection of irrelevance of logical arguments to faith
sola gratia objection
objection that the cure is worse than the disease
lifestyle apologetics

7

DOING APOLOGETICS WELL

In the previous two chapters I attempted to answer what I termed in-principle objections to Christian apologetics—objections to the very idea of Christian apologetics. I now turn to the matter of as-practiced objections—objections to the way apologetics has been done. While it is impossible to deny that Christians have practiced apologetics in both ineffective and inappropriate ways, it is possible to sketch a different picture, a picture of apologetics done well. That is the task of this chapter.

Doing apologetics well requires three things. First, one's arguments must be effective. They must be logically valid and persuasive, and they must directly address the objections offered by skeptics. Second, one must have a proper conceptualization of the nature of both Christian belief and unbelief. In other words, an apologist must properly understand both the reasons why people do not believe in the Christian God and what mature belief in God should look like. Third, and most important, one's attitude and approach to apologetic conversations must be appropriate. Too often, Christians have been condescending, arrogant and dismissive in their apologetic encounters. In other words, Christian apologists have approached apologetic situations in ways that stand in stark contrast to the attitude Jesus took when engaging those who were skeptical of his message. When one's attitude and approach are inappropriate, the results are devastating. Not only does it undercut the potential strength of one's arguments; an inappropriate approach reinforces the negative perception of both Christian apologetics and the Christian gospel message. There is a lot riding on getting this right.

Too often, Christians have been condescending, arrogant and dismissive in their apologetic encounters.

Think of Christian apologetics as a journey. Whenever you want to go someplace, you must know three things: where you are, where you want to go and how to get from where you are to where you want to go; or, in other words, you must know your origin and your destination, and you must have proper directions. Getting any of these things wrong will result in getting lost, ending up in the wrong destination. In real life, this is a minor annoyance, requiring one to pull over and ask directions. In the apologetic journey, getting lost can have eternal consequences.

In our analogy, the origin of the journey is the unbelieving mindset of the apologist's conversation partner. In order to help a partner address his or her objections to Christianity, one must understand why the partner does not already embrace Christianity. The destination is, of course, full-fledged Christian belief. In order to be sure that it is actually full-fledged Christian belief that is being defended and commended, the apologist must be sure to avoid setting the bar either too high or too low. Finally, in our journey analogy, the turn-by-turn directions represent the actual encounter, including the quality of one's arguments and the approach and attitude to the entire conversation. Consequently, in this chapter we will focus on three things: (1) a proper understanding of the nature of Christian belief, (2) a proper understanding of the nature of unbelief and (3) combining a proper approach to apologetic conversations with effective apologetic arguments.

I. THE NATURE OF CHRISTIAN BELIEF

One of the most important aspects of an appropriate and effective apologetic is a proper conceptualization of the nature of religious belief itself. Those who think that religious belief is nothing more than possessing the right evidence will naturally construe apologetics in a way that exclusively involves marshaling evidence for Christianity and against other worldviews. On the other hand, those who think that Christian belief involves only a set of ethical or (to misuse a term quite badly) practical commitments will either reject apologetics outright or see it only as a suggestion of a particular way to live a good life. While Christianity is a worldview or a system of beliefs, it is more than just that. More accurately, the Christian worldview is a system of beliefs that entails actions, values and commitments. In other words, Christianity is a holistic system of belief that involves all of a person: mind, heart and hands. This means that any attempt to reduce Christian belief to one or another aspect of life will be problematic. For Christian apologetics to be effective, it must address the intellectual component of Christian belief. But for Christian apologetics to be appropriate, for it to do justice to the truths of Christianity, it must be acknowledged that Christian belief exists not merely for the sake of knowing truths but for the sake of relational transformation of people into the image of Jesus Christ.

While it is, of course, impossible to fully consider the nature of the Christian belief system, given that our focus is on understanding the task of Christian apologetics, it is possible to focus on three fundamental questions. The Christian apologist must have a proper conceptualization of (1) what it means to say that Christian beliefs are true, (2) what we are attempting to do when we argue for Christian beliefs and (3) what the ultimate reason for having true Christian belief is.

What is meant when we say Christian beliefs are true? When a Christian apologist defends a particular Christian belief (such as "Jesus is the Son of God"), the goal is not merely to suggest that the belief is pragmatically useful or persuasive or spiritually fruitful. The apologist is claiming that the belief "Jesus is the Son of God" is true. Moreover, the understanding of *true* is not merely "true for me" or "true for my culture or race or denomination." The claim is that the Christian belief in question is true in a more robust sense, in the sense of "describing what is." Philosophers have labeled this understanding of truth the *correspondence theory of truth* because it understands truth as a relation between statements (such as "Jesus is the Son of God") and reality.

One must understand two things about this conceptualization of truth. First, it is extremely difficult to deny. It expresses the common, everyday understanding of what it means when somebody says that "X is true." And alternative accounts of truth either lead to blatantly contradictory outcomes or are parasitic on the correspondence theory of truth. Second, despite the centrality of the correspondence theory of truth to our thinking, this understanding of truth is, to put it mildly, a bit unpopular in contemporary culture. That fact alone, however, should not send the Christian apologist back to the drawing board, looking for an account of truth that causes those in contemporary society less intellectual indigestion. It is, after all, quite possible that it is contemporary culture that has the problem here, not the correspondence theory of truth.

But some of the fault here lies at the feet of Christian apologists who, in their sincere desire to present the strongest possible case for Christian belief, have presented a naive and overly simplistic picture of what it means to say that a statement corresponds to reality. Christians have too often dismissed the complexities associated with descriptions of reality and downplayed the role their perspective plays in their descriptions. As I discussed in chapter five, many

descriptive truth claims involve "socially acceptable approximation." It is acceptable to describe one's height as five feet eleven
inches even though one is a few hundredths of an inch less than
that and to describe one's age as thirty-seven even though one's
birthday was more than seven months ago. Such descriptions are
true because they fit within commonly accepted norms of approximation. Consequently, one who desires to defend the idea that there
is a correspondence between our statements and reality must acknowledge that our descriptive statements are never perfectly precise representations of the reality we describe. Our descriptions assume a particular perspective and are articulated with particular
purposes. In this way, our descriptive statements are like maps.[1]

Maps are designed to appropriately represent reality, but do so
with a particular set of purposes and given a particular set of assumptions. They typically highlight some features of reality such
as the course of rivers and highways but ignore others; the pollu-
tion from the local power plant is omitted, as is the seemingly
ubiquitous traffic on the highway. Similarly, while a map provides
a generally adequate description of, say, the shoreline of a lake, it
is never a perfect mirror of reality. Minute details and deviations
are omitted. But none of this suggests that details of maps are
purely socially constructed or open to change if a majority of people desire it. For example, a map that places Houston, Texas, in
the middle of Canada is a poor representation of the reality it pur-
ports to describe. And while a majority of citizens of International
Falls, Minnesota, might desire to relocate to Bora Bora, drawing a
map and placing northern Minnesota in the middle of French
Polynesia won't do the trick.

The application of this cartographic metaphor for truth to religious beliefs is relatively straightforward. The goal of theology is
to create a map of beliefs that adequately describes God's nature,
desires, actions and expectations of human beings. And our theological descriptions of God are true when they adequately repre-

sent divine reality. Of course, no particular statement will describe God completely or perfectly. Even statements like "God is love" are made from a particular perspective and take on the limitations of that perspective—it is false to say "God is love" if by "love" you mean nothing more than "has warm feelings for me" or if by "God" you mean "Satan." Moreover, nobody holds that they can fully understand God's love. But the failure to *fully* understand something doesn't mean that you don't understand it *truly*. More generally, the point is this: Acknowledging that human religious knowledge is limited and perspectival does nothing to undercut the idea that true descriptions of religious reality are possible. And the fact that our religious beliefs are grounded in reality is crucially important. As Nancey Murphy has said, "If theological beliefs are not grounded in facts—facts about who God is and what he has done—then they are mere fairy tales, however comforting they may be."[2] And while one may learn from fairy tales, in the final analysis, one cannot truly commit to or be comforted by them. This is why the goal of apologetics is to recommend and defend what is true about the Christian faith while acknowledging the complexities of the concept of truth and its application to religious beliefs.

> The goal of theology is to create a map of beliefs that adequately describes God's nature, desires, actions and expectations of human beings.

What are we doing when we argue for Christian beliefs? Are apologetic arguments intended to be proofs? Does the logical validity of apologetic arguments even really matter? These questions are crucially important. I argue that intellectual arguments do really matter; the Christian faith should be based on sound intellectual reasons. Proof (in one sense of that word), however, is neither possible nor desirable and therefore should not be the goal of apologetics.

In taking this stance, I am attempting to steer a middle road between two powerful factions in contemporary Christianity. The first is some variety of *fideism*, which involves the claim that Christian belief is not based on intellectual arguments and reasons. The second is some variety of *rationalism*, which involves the notion that it is only possible to assert a belief as true if one can provide a proof for that belief. Both of these are seductive. In rejecting the need for intellectual grounding, fideism protects religious belief from intellectual refutation, and in demanding proof, rationalism (supposedly) provides the means to demonstrate that one's beliefs are certain and that one's competitors' beliefs are false. These supposed advantages, however, come at a high cost.

The problem with fideism is this: Intellectual reasons are certainly not irrelevant to Christian belief. While it is doubtful that anybody's conversion has been purely intellectual, it is also doubtful that intellectual reasons and arguments have ever been completely absent from a conversion experience. While fideism is motivated by an understandable desire to avoid an intellectual reductionism of the Christian faith, in their desire to avoid intellectual reductionism, fideists go too far and ignore the role of the intellect in making fundamental worldview decisions. Separating religious belief from the intellect does not protect Christian belief; it makes it intellectually irrelevant. And an intellectually irrelevant faith cannot be taught to the next generation. Since God created humans with inquiring minds, this irrelevance is a profound barrier to Christian commitment.

Rationalists, on the other hand, take the reasonable affirmation of the importance of rational arguments to an unreasonable extreme. They argue that merely basing Christian belief on reasons is inadequate. After all, it is possible for other worldviews to give reasons too. What is needed, they argue, is proof. Of course, the plausibility of this requirement depends on what is meant by proof. There is a vague, everyday notion of proof that is achieved rather easily. Anything you can provide a good argument for is proved in this sense. Another notion of proof is found in mathematics. Here it is possible to demonstrate that a particular conclusion follows necessarily from particular premises given the assumption of a particular set of axioms. But *mathematical proof* does not and cannot demonstrate the truthfulness of the premises and axioms. The strictest notion of proof is one that I will call *philosophical proof*. Philosophical proof of a proposition A is achieved when one can demonstrate that not-A is impossible. For example, I can prove that I am sitting right now if and only if I can demonstrate that my perception of this aspect of reality is accurate and that I cannot be mistaken, misinformed or misled in any way. Philosophical proof places its holder in the strongest possible epistemological position. The rationalist's demand for proof is typically expressed in terms of philosophical proof. A rationalist objects that everyday and mathematical proof fail to provide a requisite degree of certainty because they do not rule out the possibility that you could be wrong.

There are two possible responses to the rationalist's demand for philosophical proof. The first is simply to deny that such proof is possible; the second is to go further and argue that even if proof were possible it would be antithetical to the very concept of Christian belief. While I will focus on the first of these objections, I am also very sympathetic with the second. The search for absolute proof is closely correlated with the very problematic assertion, "I will submit to God and believe his revelation only under these conditions." The attitude behind the demand for absolute proof is probably idolatrous and/or involves an inappropriate assumption about either what God must do in revealing himself or what humans can do themselves in coming to know God. Nonetheless, I will focus on the first response to the demand for proof—arguing that proof is impossible—because, after all, if proof is not possible, then the objection to the demand for proof might be interesting for theological reasons, but would still be practically irrelevant.

Is proof of Christian beliefs possible? Everyday and maybe even mathematical proofs of Christian beliefs are relatively easy. There are good arguments for Christian belief, and if certain assumptions are granted, one might even be able to demonstrate (in some sense of that term) God's existence. But how about philosophical proof? Is philosophical proof of Christian beliefs possible? In a word, no. Of course, this should not be too troubling for Christians because philosophical proof is elusive even in apparently obvious cases. In most circumstances, when I look out the window and see a tree, I am quite confident that I am seeing a real tree and that my eyesight is not deceiving me. But do I have a proof that there is a tree? No, because even if it seems obvious that I see a tree, I could be wrong. The circumstances in which our beliefs are formed play a pivotal role. If it is dark or if I have mistakenly ingested a hallucinogen that causes me to see things that are not there, or if I know that my friends are running around projecting holograms of trees in an attempt to make their neighborhood seem more lush and appealing than it actually is, then, to the degree that I am aware of these things, I will be more cautious about my belief. But even if there are no circumstances of which I am aware that would suggest that I am mistaken with respect to my belief that I see a tree, I still don't have a proof that the tree exists. This is because there are a host of logically possible (even if extremely unlikely) scenarios that could result in misleading information about the tree outside my window. I could, in fact, be a denizen of the Matrix, and if so, the tree would be merely a construct of a program; I could be deceived by a powerful, malevolent demon intent on causing as much intel-

> *Is philosophical proof of Christian beliefs possible? In a word, no.*

lectual confusion as possible; and so on.

But doesn't my inability to prove the existence of the tree mean that I don't really know that the tree exists? No. It is possible that my belief is true and perfectly reasonable even though I cannot provide a philosophical proof of it. The simple fact of the matter is that I have good reasons for believing that I am not a denizen of the Matrix and that my friends do not possess the ability to project holograms. Moreover, I am justified in believing that my eyesight (and associated cognitive apparatus) is reliable with respect to tree-sized objects. Given these assumptions, I will rightly assume that my eyesight is generally capable of providing true beliefs. In such a case, the conviction that I do, in fact, see a tree is perfectly reasonable and, I would argue, can be considered knowledge. Of course, this suggests that our knowledge claims are to some degree provisional. We must acknowledge the possibility of error. But this implies fallibilism, not skepticism. We must admit that we are not God; we are not forced to admit that there is no God. The lesson here is that the possibility of error undercuts knowledge only given the assumption that knowledge requires absolute proof and certainty. Absolute proof is not possible, but that fact does nothing to undercut or even diminish the role of rational arguments for Christian belief.

What then is the role of intellectual arguments in the Christian faith? Intellectual arguments can provide additional support to religious belief that was reached in other ways, such as through testimony or personal experience. Intellectual arguments can deflect (at least partially) objections to the faith such as the problem of evil or the objection to the possibility of miracles. And arguments can expose and remove inconsistencies in one's theological belief system and thereby create a more secure, coherent religious worldview. It is important to note, however, that it is likely that the intellectual aspect of Christian belief will play a different role in different people's belief systems. Some people have a very high need for reasons, others have less. The point relevant to fideism, however, is that nobody has no need for reasons. On the other hand, neither is it the case that the Christian faith is based wholly and completely on rational arguments and reasons. Even those with an extreme need to understand and prove the Christian faith must assume certain things without supporting arguments. Those who have really delved deeply into theological questions will realize that there is some point at which rational arguments either cease to function or cease to be persuasive. Consequently, very few mature Christians will say that they believe in God because of an argument for God's existence. Some of the justification or warrant Christians possess for their religious beliefs may very likely come from rational arguments, but—again, for mature Christians—the basis of their religious belief will be related to experiencing God's presence in prayer and in Christian community, through participating in Christian sacraments and rituals and the like. But the fact that religious arguments are not the primary basis for religious belief does not suggest in any way that they are irrelevant to apologetics.

William Lane Craig makes a nice distinction between knowing the faith to be true and showing the faith to be true.[3] Since apologetics is about defending and commending the faith—in other words, showing the faith to be true—the attempt to give the reasons for the hope that Christians have in Christ will inevitably and fittingly involve offering arguments, evidences and reasons.

What is the ultimate goal of having true Christian beliefs? Some Christian apologists have been guilty of seeing the possession of true beliefs as an end in itself. Truth is important, and apologetics is about defending the truthfulness of Christian belief. But Christianity does not exist solely as a set of true beliefs. It is fundamentally a way of being, living, acting and doing. It might be said that Christianity is always and irreducibly practical. James 2:19 powerfully makes the point that belief alone is insufficient: "You believe that God is one; well and good. Even the demons believe that—and tremble with fear" (NET). Satan undoubtedly has many correct theological beliefs—his problem is not theological, but affectional. His problem is that he hates God and what God stands for.

Christianity necessarily includes an intellectual dimension, an affectional dimension and a practical dimension. In other words, Christianity requires the full action of the head, heart and hands. For example, consider the belief "God wants me to share the gospel with those who don't know him." It is perfectly possible to fully understand this true belief and do nothing about it. Belief without action is impotent. But the opposite is equally problematic. Merely acting without an understanding of God's nature, will and desires is not likely to produce a positive result.

> Christianity requires the full action of the head, heart and hands.

Since Christian belief is not merely about the accumulation of theological trivia, apologetics cannot focus solely on helping people believe true things about God. To do so is to sanction either implicitly or explicitly an unbiblical intellectual reductionism. But we must be careful to avoid the opposite extreme as well. My claim is that Christian beliefs should entail commitment and action, not that commitment and action are more important than or even are separable from belief. While it is inappropriate to dwell only on belief and truth, it is equally problematic to eliminate or even disparage the rational component of Christianity and dwell only on the commitment and action.

If Christian belief necessarily includes belief, commitment and action, does this suggest that apologetics must not only seek to defend belief but also seek to induce commitment and encourage action? No. To explain this we need to make a distinction between what apologetics defends and what apologetics is. Apologetics defends Christian belief, but it is not itself identical with Christian belief. Apologetics is the act of defending and commending the Christian faith. While the apologist must be careful to defend true Christian belief—an understanding of Christianity with an intimate connection between belief, commitment and action—apologetics itself is not primarily concerned about inducing commitment and encouraging action. That does not suggest that these things are unimportant, only that they are not a part of the apologetic enterprise. As we discussed in the last chapter, some find in this an objection to apologetics: If it does not induce commitment and encourage action, then it is not authentically Christian. This objection is misguided. Of course, if apologetics discourages commitment and action, then there is a real problem. But there is no problem if Christian apologetics focuses on the rational dimension of faith as long as it acknowledges that the rational dimension is only doing part of what Christianity is. In this respect, the apologist is like a contractor that builds the foundation of a house. It would be silly to build a foundation and think that the house was complete, but it would be equally misguided to say that because the contractor only builds foundations (and not the walls and roof) that this contractor's work is unnecessary or irrelevant to the process of constructing a house.

2. THE NATURE OF UNBELIEF

While properly understanding the nature of belief is very important, so is understanding the other side of the equation: the nature of unbelief. The term *unbelief,* however, applies to a variety of perspectives. These perspectives are different in many respects but share a common rejection of the truth of Christian belief. First, there are a small number of *committed atheists* who have considered the objections for and against the existence of God and have come to believe that God does not exist and that therefore all religious traditions are, at their core, false. Emboldened by the "new atheism" of Richard Dawkins, Daniel Dennett, Sam Harris and Christopher Hitchens, committed atheists are increasingly evangelistic about their beliefs. Second, there are *agnostics* who, for one reason or another, do not really know what to think about the idea of religious belief. Some agnostics have thought through religious issues carefully and have decided that there is not enough evidence to really believe either "God exists" or "God does not exist"—much like the stance most people take toward whether there is life elsewhere in the universe. Other agnostics (probably the vast majority) are less thoughtful. They aren't sure what to think about religions so they avoid situations that would require them to think about their religious beliefs (or lack thereof). Third, there are *adherents of other religious traditions*. These are, of course, neither atheists nor agnostics, but they nonetheless find traditional Christianity to be false. Finally, there are what I will call *nonrealist Christians*. Nonrealist Christians accept that Christianity is true in some sense of the word, but not in the sense that it represents the way religious reality really is. A nonrealist Christian would accept the label "Christian" only because it is the religious tradition in which they were raised or because they believe that it is life-guiding or useful to think that Jesus is the Son of God even while rejecting that the historical person Jesus was actually fully divine, was resurrected, etc. Included under the category of nonrealist Christians are religious pluralists who believe that all religions are true or salvific—in effect, all religious roads lead to God. To make this claim, they must reject the truthfulness of anything that is unique or exclusive about all religious traditions, including Christianity.

Under the influence of modernism, it has commonly been thought that unbelief was primarily the result of failing to have the right arguments. The list of *intellectual causes of unbelief* is long and distinguished. The problem of evil, the existence of other world religions, the objection that religious belief lacks evidence,

Freud's objection to religious belief as wish fulfillment, Feuerbach's objection to religious belief as projection, and objections to the reliability or historicity of Scripture have all had places of prominence in the atheological hall of fame. Consequently, answering these (and other) objections has understandably been the primary focus of Christian apologetics. While this is appropriate as part of the picture, it is not sufficient because the intellectual dimension is only one of the causes of unbelief. And it is likely that it is not even the most influential or common. In addition to these intellectual objections to Christian belief, there are what I will call affective causes and spiritual causes of unbelief.

While intellectual causes of unbelief occur when there are unresolved intellectual objections to Christianity, *affective causes of unbelief* are the result of being wounded or having unresolved personal pain associated with Christian belief. Sadly, this is all too common and could happen in any number of ways. A person who has been physically, sexually or emotionally abused by a person with spiritual authority will likely (and understandably) reject the religious beliefs of that authority figure. This is almost certain if, as is too often the case, the authority figure seeks to justify or explain his or her actions in terms of religious beliefs. Affective objections to Christian belief might occur even if a person has not personally experienced pain or abuse. It is often enough to look around and see others in pain or being abused. In fact, an affective objection to Christian belief might even occur in the absence of profound pain and suffering. Whenever there is a gap between expectations and reality, an affective objection is possible. Suppose one is raised in a religious tradition that claims that if God really loves you, then you will experience wealth and health. Those who do not receive these promised blessings will likely interpret their experiences as the result of either a lack of faith on their part or a lack of love for them on God's part. In either case, they are likely to develop an affective objection to Christian belief.

In addition to intellectual and affective causes of unbelief, there are *spiritual causes of unbelief.* A spiritual cause of unbelief occurs when one is unable or unwilling to submit to Jesus Christ. Christian belief amounts to, among other things, an acknowledgment of Jesus Christ as Lord of one's life. Submission to Christ includes acknowledging the authority of his revelation and submitting to what he has revealed about human purposes, actions and destinations. And this is simply much more than some people are willing to do. Original sin has made selfishness a common commodity in human beings (sadly, not just in nonbelievers!), and complete submission (to anything or anybody) is not something that fits well with a life characterized by selfishness. Take for example, my friend John (name changed). John knows that he routinely engages in self-destructive behavior, and he knows that there are good arguments and reasons for Christian belief. His objection to Christianity, if you can call it that, is that he doesn't want to change his life. In an interesting way, there is something praiseworthy about that. Unlike many, John realizes that an authentic commitment to Christianity is life changing. Sadly, his decision is to maintain the status quo, to maintain his lordship over his life and to continue his self-destructive behavior.

Of course, intellectual, affective and spiritual causes of unbelief are not neatly segregated. It is extremely likely that those who reject Christianity do so for more than one and probably even all of these reasons. Whatever the cause of unbelief, the fundamental result is a lack of *basic trust* when approaching Christian belief. Whether it be because of an unanswered objection to Christianity, pain or hurt, or a desire for autonomy, some people have a default setting of mistrust toward Christianity. Of course, this mistrust manifests itself in different ways. When people focus on their intellectual objections, their *basic mistrust* comes out as "there is not enough evidence" or "this doesn't make sense." When they focus on their affective objections, it comes out as a desire to protect themselves from hurt or as an inability to trust, and when they focus on their spiritual objection, it manifests as "Who are you to tell me how I should live?"

This attitude of basic trust and mistrust is of crucial importance. Christian belief is unique in that its essential beliefs are not mundane beliefs like "I see a tree." My attitude and approach do not typically affect whether I acknowledge whether there is a tree in front of me. But in the case of belief in God, attitude and approach matter. Whether it be looking at arguments for God's existence or answers to the problem of evil, it makes a big difference whether you approach the matter

> *Whatever the cause of unbelief, the fundamental result is a lack of basic trust when approaching Christian belief.*

with basic trust—an openness to and even a desire for the truth of God's existence—or basic mistrust—a skeptical "you must prove it to me or else" sort of approach. Notice that belief in God isn't completely unique in this respect, however, because something like this is similar in deciding whether one will love and trust another person. The task of apologetics, therefore, is to acknowledge the multiplicity of reasons that might motivate a person's distrust toward the gospel of Jesus Christ and offer them sound arguments for the reasonability of a stance of basic trust.

3. HOW TO APPROACH APOLOGETIC SITUATIONS

Suppose you have an accurate picture of both why people reject Christianity and what Christian belief is. What is lacking is an understanding of how to help encourage people to move from unbelief to belief, from mistrust to trust, from rejection to commitment. This is crucially important because history is filled with examples of Christian apologists who have done this poorly or inappropriately. In their desire to persuade, Christian apologists have too often used methods that undercut the gospel they are defending and commending. The disastrous effects of inappropriate apologetic efforts have caused many to reject the viability of apologetics and suggest that persuasion is not something Christians should engage in. Consequently, the very viability of apologetics depends on finding a way to engage in defense and persuasion that do not offend the gospel we are defending. To that end, I offer six principles for effective and appropriate apologetics.

Principle 1: The quality of your arguments matters. The first principle is perhaps the most obvious. The idea is clear and practically undeniable: People generally are not persuaded by sloppy reasoning and fallacious arguments. And if they are, they probably should not be, for if a person is persuaded that Christianity is true for bad reasons, the faith that grows out of those reasons is likely to wither.

Developing a good apologetic argument is not easy. What is required is, first, a substantial knowledge of Scripture and theology. Passion and conviction are important, but there is no substitute for careful study and careful research. Second, developing a good argument for the faith requires a willingness to strip away faulty arguments and reasoning by truly testing, prodding and probing the intellectual viability of one's most cherished religious beliefs. This requires courage and confidence. People who are afraid that their beliefs might turn out to be false are people who will never truly test those beliefs, and, consequently, they will likely have only superficial reasons for their beliefs. Third, good apologetic arguments must consider all the available evidence rather than just some selected portion of it. One who looks at only the evidence that is comfortable and conducive to one's current beliefs will develop arguments that are only convincing to those who share one's beliefs and ignorance. Fourth, good apologetic arguments preemptively deal with potential objections. And when one considers what sorts of objections might be raised to one's arguments, it is crucial to consider the strongest form of those objections rather than watered-down, easily dismissible versions of them. Finally, the presentation of apologetic arguments should match the educational and intellectual level of one's interlocutor. It is demeaning to give a first-grade argument to a person with a Ph.D., and it is foolish to give Ph.D. arguments to a first grader. Finding the right level of presentation is not easy, but it is important.

Principle 2: Who you are is more important than what you say. Apologetics has traditionally been cast exclusively as the marshaling of arguments for Christianity. While arguments and their persuasiveness are important, the character of the person making the argument is more important. It is obvious that people are more likely to accept the truth of what is said by a person that is perceived to be honest as opposed to a person who is perceived to be dishonest. The same may be said of a person who is perceived to be knowledgeable rather than ignorant, genuine rather than manipulative, and humble rather than arrogant.

I'm not saying that if an apologist is a person of character, his bad arguments magically become good arguments. Rather, I am saying that if a person is arrogant and dismissively close-minded, it will not matter how good his or her arguments are for they will likely be dismissed without a real hearing. In other words, being a person of character is a necessary part of being an effective apologist, but it is not sufficient by itself. If an apologist is a person of character, then the character itself functions as a kind of an argument for the truth of Christianity. It provides a positive example of the effects of basic trust toward the gospel of Jesus Christ. To paraphrase Francis of Assisi, who once famously said, "Go into the world and share the gospel, and use words if necessary," apologists should "go into the world to defend and commend the gospel, and use words and actions that are commensurate with the gospel you defend."

Consequently, while intelligence and knowledge are important for an apologist, having a high IQ (intelligence quotient) is probably less essential (although certainly not irrelevant) than having a high EQ (emotional quotient) and RQ (relational quotient). Being comfortable with who you are, being able to control your emotions, and having a natural ability to connect with and relate to people are absolutely essential skills for effective and appropriate apologetics. In fact, if you lack people skills and emotional health, the clearest way you can benefit the Christian faith is to not do apologetics, even if you have a high IQ and an excellent grasp of apologetic arguments.

Principle 3: It's not about you. The third principle of apologetics is an extension of the first. One of the most common ways would-be Christian apologists fail in their attempt to defend the gospel in a Christlike manner is that they make the apologetic encounter about themselves, rather than about their conversation partner. In so doing, Christian apologists lose sight of the ultimate goal for all Christians—showing Christ's love to a world who needs to see it. Sometimes Christian apologists have a primary or secondary goal to impress their conversation partners with their religious knowledge. Other times, their desire is to impress other Christians who may be listening with their apologetic and evangelistic zeal. Most commonly, however, Christian apologists fall into the trap of competitiveness and see the conversation as an opportunity to win a game of intellectual and theological chess.

It really isn't that difficult to "win" an apologetic argument. You can get sarcastic, dismissive, intimidating or simply dishonest with the facts. But the goal of apologetics cannot be to merely win an argument. Those who try to win an apologetic argument at all costs find themselves in the unfortunate situation of winning a battle but losing the war. This is, of course, much easier said than done. When one's conversation partner gets sarcastic and dismissive, it is only human to want to join the partner in the gutter for a nice bout of mudslinging. The problem is that how you defend Christ really matters. There are many times in apologetics situations where you need to turn the other cheek and overlook disparaging, unfair or sarcastic comments. This is not easy, but it is essential.

One of the most important antidotes to falling into competitiveness or self-aggrandizement is humor, especially appropriately self-deprecating humor. Too many Christian apologists transfer the seriousness of the task of defending Christian belief to their approach to defending Christian belief. In so doing, they tend to take themselves more seriously than they should. Yes, the task of sharing and defending the gospel is incredibly important and needs to be taken seriously, but there are few things more toxic to a thought-

Take the gospel seriously, not yourself.

ful and effective apologetic conversation than an artificial level of intense seriousness and urgency. Nobody wants to be preached at. Take the gospel seriously, not yourself.

Principle 4: It is about them. If an apologetic encounter is not about the apologist, then (fairly obviously) it is about the conversation partner. To be effective, apologetics must be contextual or *audience focused.* It is difficult to underestimate the importance of this point. This audience focus should be manifested in (at least) five different ways.

First, we must be aware of the uniqueness of particular relational situations, and we should seek an apologetic approach that is appropriate to that particular situation. A conversation with siblings, roommates, parents, an older or younger person, or a person of a different gender each has a very different relational dynamic. Generally speaking, people are resistant to hearing critiques of their beliefs from their siblings. Similarly, parents are often resistant to the suggestion that their children know something that they do not. Apologetic conversations with people older and younger than you also have unique relational dynamics. Older people may be resistant to being corrected by a younger person, and younger people often react negatively to anything they interpret as condescension. And apologetic conversations between men and women are complicated by the differences in gender, not to mention the additional relational complexities associated with conversations between two unmarried people of similar age. Finally, there are also important cultural factors that must be taken into account in apologetic conversations. For example, some cultures approach historical arguments with greater skepticism; others place a great deal of emphasis on honoring one's family by maintaining family traditions and beliefs; still others deem it to be very impolite to strike up a conversation without first introducing yourself. Effective apologetics requires being aware of these potential cultural pitfalls.

Second, an audience-focused approach should affect the way we explain our Christian beliefs and the way we see their religious beliefs. We need to focus on their questions, their story. A preplanned, prepackaged, one-size-fits-all apologetic presentation is more than likely to miss the mark completely. As discussed in chapter six, when Luke says to those who would be witnesses to the gospel of Jesus Christ, "Be resolved not to rehearse ahead of time how to make your defense" in Luke 21:14 (NET), he is objecting to a canned, preplanned presentation that ignores the perspective of the interlocutor and the leading of the Holy Spirit. We must also take our interlocutor's beliefs seriously. We should not assume up-front that they are misinformed or misguided. We should even see the apologetic conversation as a real opportunity to learn. Understanding the beliefs of those who disagree with us and understanding why they disagree with us helps us better understand our own beliefs. In other words, in our apologetic conversations, Christian apologists need to be able to strike the right balance between openness and conviction. There is a real sense in which we can be open to the beliefs of our conversation partner. But our openness can never come at the expense of conviction. We can value others' beliefs and even learn from them without diminishing the conviction with which we hold our Christian belief.

Third, an audience-focused approach to apologetics should affect the language we use in our conversations. As much as possible we should avoid Christian-speak like "born again," "saved by the blood" and "slain in the Spirit." This sort of language is (at least sometimes) fine for conversations between Christians, but when talking to those outside the circle of faith, we should seek to translate. Even when having conversations with Christians or those only moderately familiar with Christian language and culture, it is important to seek to translate our ideas into clearer speech. This has been well said by C. S. Lewis:

> We must learn the language of our audience. And let me say at the outset that it is no use at all laying down *a priori* what the "plain man" does or does not understand. You have to find out by experience. . . . You must translate every bit of your theology into the vernacular. This is very troublesome, . . . but it is essential. It is also of the greatest service to your own thought. I have come to the conclusion that if you cannot translate your thoughts into uneducated language, then your thoughts are confused. Power to translate is the test of having really understood your own meaning.[4]

Fourth, an audience-focused approach to apologetics should affect how we see ourselves. The natural but mistaken assumption is that our interlocutor sees us as we see ourselves. We may tacitly acknowledge that non-Christians see Christians as arrogant and narrow-minded, but override that belief by reminding ourselves: "Of course, that's not me; I'm not arrogant and narrow-minded." The problem is that, at least with respect to apologetic conversations, in an important sense perception is reality. As David Clark says, a Christian apologist "should be aware that . . . I am not myself at least at first, I am what the dialogue partner thinks I am."[5] You might be the most humble person on the planet, but your conversation partner might only know you as a Christian and might therefore view you as "one of those know-it-all Christian-types." Consequently, Christian apologists need to develop what I will call empathic vision. You need to see yourself as your inter-locutor sees you. Only when you understand how you are viewed will you be able to seek to rehabilitate the image of Christians (and, by extension, you) that your unbelieving friend brings to the table.

Finally, an audience-centered approach to apologetics means that listening is more important than speaking, and understanding is more than being understood. Only if we listen carefully will we be able to see ourselves as our conversation partner sees us. Only if we listen carefully will we have a chance of answering the questions and objections that they are really asking rather than the questions we would be asking if we were them. And only if we listen carefully will we have a chance of demonstrating to them in a tangible way that we value them as persons and take their beliefs seriously even if we disagree with them. Being knowledgeable is a great thing, but it is not the only thing. Sadly, too often, the more knowledgeable a Christian, the greater the temptation to treat apologetic encounters as opportunities to dispense information and knowledge. This is not only unhelpful; it is often dangerous. A Christian apologist who speaks without listening unintentionally reinforces the negative stereotype of Christians as pushy, know-it-all jerks.

> *Listening is more important than speaking, and understanding is more than being understood.*

And this is devastating because for many people this stereotype is one of the most significant barriers to faith. One might say that an apologist who has lots of knowledge but lacks the desire to listen and understand is like a car that has five hundred horsepower but no steering wheel. It will go really fast, but it will be out of control and a danger to everybody in the vicinity.

Principle 5: Set the correct goal. One of the reasons it is difficult to follow through on the idea that we should allow our conversation partner's questions and objections to drive the conversation is the notion that the goal of every apologetic conversation is to convert our conversation partner. If that is the goal, we feel the need to steer the conversation and push the other person to a place where we can "pop the question." Without denying that there are instances in which Christians need to be courageous and encourage unbelievers to commit their lives to Christ, generally speaking, the notion that every conversation needs to end with an altar call is profoundly problematic. It is this goal that fuels the perception of Christians as pushy, arrogant and only interested in people if they are willing to convert and join the club. The question "Can I convert her or him?" is the wrong question. The right question is "Can I, by my arguments, attitude and actions, move her or him a step closer to relationship with Jesus Christ?"

This can be accomplished in a number of ways. Most obviously, Christian apologists can offer sound positive reasons to think Christianity is true and seek to overcome intellectual objections that serve as barriers to embracing Christian belief. Less obvious, but equally important, however, is the task of transforming negative Christian stereotypes. The most common reason people reject Christianity is not an intellectual objection but a disapproval of Christians themselves. Brennan Manning said this well: "The greatest single cause of atheism today is Christians who acknowledge Jesus with their lips and then walk out the door and deny Him with their lifestyle. That is what an unbelieving world simply finds unbelievable."[6] Consequently, one of the most important things Christian apologists can do is help non-Christians realize that not all Christians are like their negative stereotypes. In other words, we need to act in such a way as to refute their stereotypes. We need to show that they are not accurate descriptions of Christians, Christianity or Christ.

Principle 6: Acknowledge the role of the Holy Spirit. Our final principle for effective and appropriate apologetics is no less important just because it comes last. It is, in fact, arguably the most important principle. In our apologetic encounters, we must see ourselves as part of a process—a process in which the most important player is not us, but the Holy Spirit. As apologists we must baptize all our apologetic endeavors in the conviction that unless the Holy Spirit has prepared the ground for our conversation, is with us in our conversation, and will continue the work of conviction long after the conversation is ended, our efforts will come to nothing. In other words, apologetics involves planting seeds that only the Holy Spirit can water, nurture and guide to germination. Without this conviction it is too easy to fall into the idea that apologetic success is determined wholly by our performance. And that idea too often yields a crop of pushy, arrogant and decidedly un-Christlike apologetics.

> *In our apologetic encounters, we must see ourselves as part of a process—a process in which the most important player is not us, but the Holy Spirit.*

To this end, it is crucially important to pray both for those we will speak with and for ourselves. We pray for others in the hope that the Holy Spirit will protect them from our errors in speech or action, and we pray for ourselves that we will take full and appropriate advantage of all of the apologetic opportunities given us by the Spirit. In his classic *Power Through Prayer,* E. M. Bounds said:

"No learning can make up for the failure to pray. No earnestness, no diligence, no study, no gifts will supply its lack."[7]

Reliance on the Holy Spirit is essential for another, less obvious reason. If apologists keep it firmly in the center of their attention that they are not responsible for the ultimate success of their arguments, they will be protected from "buying their own hype" or falling into the trap of seeing their faith as the sort of thing that can be reduced to intellectual argument. C. S. Lewis draws our attention to this potential danger:

> I have found that nothing is more dangerous to one's faith than the work of an apologist. No doctrine of that Faith seems so spectral, so unreal as one that I have just successfully defended in a public debate. For a moment, you see, it has seemed to rest upon oneself: as a result, when you go away from that debate, it seems no stronger than that weak pillar. That is why we apologists take our lives in our hands and can be saved only by falling back continually from the web of our own arguments, as from our intellectual counters, into the Reality—from Christian apologetics into Christ Himself.[8]

In the final analysis, the task of apologetics is not all that difficult to understand. To do apologetics well, we must love people enough to place ourselves in situations where we can truly hear people's questions and help them find answers; it requires that we trust that God can use our learning, experiences and story in a way that is persuasive to others; and it requires a commitment to the life-transforming truth of the gospel of Jesus Christ. These things are simultaneously simple enough for anyone to do and difficult enough to justify a lifetime of study and practice. But those who spend their lives working on these things will, when they are old, look back on their lives and find them well spent.

KEY TERMS
correspondence theory of truth
fideism
rationalism
everyday proof
mathematical proof
philosophical proof
committed atheists
agnostics
nonrealist Christians
intellectual causes of unbelief
affective causes of unbelief
spiritual causes of unbelief
basic trust
basic mistrust
audience-focused apologetics

A BIBLIOGRAPHY OF WORKS
ON CHRISTIAN APOLOGETICS

The apologetic literature is vast and varied. Consequently, an exhaustive listing of apologetic works is not possible. But even if it were, it wouldn't be valuable. To be helpful, any such bibliography must be selective; it must separate the lucid, careful and erudite literature from the unclear, shoddy and unduly rhetorical. This task is difficult enough. Even more difficult, however, is selecting which of the many valuable works to include. An exhaustive list of even those works that are valuable contributions to the field is still beyond what can be included in a single volume. Consequently, I have narrowed the list of valuable apologetic works in three ways. First, I have selected only those works that are relatively easily available in English. There are many excellent non-English titles and many excellent semipublished or unpublished works, none of which are included in this bibliography. Second, I have included only books; the vast number of essays and articles, many of them of groundbreaking significance, have been omitted. Third, while I have included only contemporary treatments of apologetics, some of the most significant classical works of apologetics are discussed in chapters two and three. Finally, I have sought to include a broad variety of apologetic books: popular as well as scholarly works and works from a variety of apologetic and theological perspectives.

This bibliography has been divided into the following categories: (1) meta-apologetics and the history of apologetics; (2) general apologetics; (3) religious epistemology, relativism and skepticism; (4) existence of God; (5) problem of evil; (6) coherence of essential Christian doctrines; (7) biblical reliability and the historical Jesus; (8) the challenge of other religious traditions; and (9) objections to Christian belief.

The inclusion of the final category—objections to Christian belief—requires some explanation. Apologetics offers defenses of Christian faith against supposed refutations. One cannot do this well without understanding these objections themselves. Without actually reading the works of skeptics, it is all too easy to slip into simplistic responses that do not do justice to the depth and subtlety of the variety of atheological objections that exist in the contemporary world. Skeptics can be our friends. They can save us from having an unduly high opinion of our own bad arguments.

I. META-APOLOGETICS AND THE HISTORY OF APOLOGETICS

Boa, Kenneth D., and Robert M. Bowman Jr. *Faith Has Its Reasons: An Integrative Approach to Defending Christianity.* Colorado Springs: NavPress, 2001.

Bush, L. Russ. *Classical Readings in Christian Apologetics.* Grand Rapids: Academie, 1983.

Clark, David K. *Dialogical Apologetics: A Person-Centered Approach to Christian Defense.* Grand Rapids: Baker, 1993.

Cowan, Steven B., ed. *Five Views on Apologetics.* Counterpoints Series, edited by Stanley N. Gundry. Grand Rapids: Zondervan, 2000.

Dulles, Avery. *A History of Apologetics.* San Francisco: Ignatius, 2005.

Edgar, William, and K. Scott Oliphint. *Christian Apologetics Past and Present: A Primary Source Reader.* 2 vols. Wheaton, Ill.: Crossway, 2009, 2011.

Griffiths, Paul J. *An Apology for Apologetics: A Study in the Logic of Interreligious Dialogue.* Maryknoll, N.Y.: Orbis, 1991.

Hanna, Mark M. *Crucial Questions in Apologetics.* Grand Rapids: Baker, 1981.

Lewis, Gordon. *Testing Christianity's Truth Claims.* Chicago: Moody Press, 1976. Reprint, Lanham, Md.: University Press of America, 1990.

Mayers, Ronald. *Balanced Apologetics: Using Evidences and Presuppositions in Defense of the Faith.* Grand Rapids: Kregel, 1984.

Ramm, Bernard. *Varieties of Christian Apologetics.* Revised/retitled ed. Grand Rapids: Baker, 1961.

Reid, J. K. S. *Christian Apologetics.* Grand Rapids: Eerdmans, 1969.

Sire, James W. *A Little Primer on Humble Apologetics.* Downers Grove, Ill.: InterVarsity Press, 2006.

2. GENERAL APOLOGETICS

Boyd, Gregory A. *Letters from a Skeptic.* 1st ed. Colorado Springs: Chariot Victor, 1994.

Boyd, Gregory A., and Edward K. Boyd. *Letters from a Skeptic.* 2nd ed. Colorado Springs: David C. Cook, 2008.

Carnell, Edward J. *An Introduction to Christian Apologetics.* Grand Rapids: Eerdmans, 1948.

Craig, William Lane. *Reasonable Faith: Christian Truth and Apologetics.* Rev. ed. Wheaton, Ill.: Crossway, 1994.

Craig, William Lane, and Chad Meister, eds. *God Is Great, God Is Good: Why Believing in God Is Reasonable and Responsible.* Downers Grove, Ill.: InterVarsity Press, 2009.

Dyrness, William. *Christian Apologetics in a World Community.* Downers Grove, Ill.: InterVarsity Press, 1983.

Edgar, William. *Reasons of the Heart: Recovering Christian Persua-*

sion. Grand Rapids: Baker, 1996.

Evans, C. Stephen. *Why Believe? Reason and Mystery as Pointers to God.* Grand Rapids: Eerdmans, 1996.

Frame, John M. *Apologetics to the Glory of God: An Introduction.* Phillipsburg, N.J.: Presbyterian & Reformed, 1994.

Geisler, Norman. *Baker Encyclopedia of Christian Apologetics.* Grand Rapids: Baker, 1999.

Keller, Timothy. *The Reason for God: Belief in an Age of Skepticism.* New York: Dutton/Penguin, 2008.

Kreeft, Peter. *Fundamentals of the Faith: Essays in Christian Apologetics.* San Francisco: Ignatius, 1988.

Kreeft, Peter, and Ronald Tacelli. *Handbook of Christian Apologetics.* Downers Grove, Ill.: InterVarsity Press, 1994.

Lewis, C. S. *Mere Christianity.* New York: Macmillan, 1943.

Little, Paul. *Know Why You Believe.* 5th ed. Downers Grove, Ill.: InterVarsity Press, 2008.

McGrath, Alister E. *Intellectuals Don't Need God and Other Modern Myths: Building Bridges to Faith Through Apologetics.* Grand Rapids: Zondervan, 1993.

Meister, Chad. *Building Belief: Constructing Faith from the Ground Up.* Grand Rapids: Baker, 2006.

Moreland, J. P. *Scaling the Secular City: A Defense of Christianity.* Grand Rapids: Baker, 1987.

Moreland, J. P., and William Lane Craig. *Philosophical Foundations for a Christian Worldview.* Downers Grove, Ill.: InterVarsity Press, 2003.

Murray, Michael, ed. *Reason for the Hope Within.* Grand Rapids: Eerdmans, 1999.

Nicholi, Armand M. *The Question of God: C. S. Lewis and Sigmund Freud Debate God, Love, Sex, and the Meaning of Life.* New York: Free Press, 2002.

Ramm, Bernard. *A Christian Appeal to Reason.* Waco, Tex.: Word, 1977.

————. *Protestant Christian Evidences.* Chicago: Moody Press, 1953.

Schaeffer, Francis. *He Is There and He Is Not Silent.* Wheaton, Ill.: Tyndale House, 1972.

Sire, James. *Why Should Anyone Believe Anything at All?* Downers Grove, Ill.: InterVarsity Press, 1994.

Sproul, R. C. *Defending Your Faith: An Introduction to Apologetics.* Wheaton, Ill.: Crossway, 2003.

Sproul, R. C., John Gerstner and Arthur Lindsley. *Classical Apologetics: A Rational Defense of the Christian Faith and a Critique of Presuppositional Apologetics.* Grand Rapids: Zondervan, 1984.

Stackhouse, John G. *Humble Apologetics: Defending the Faith Today.* Oxford: Oxford University Press, 2002.

Strobel, Lee. *The Case for Faith.* Grand Rapids: Zondervan, 2000.

Swinburne, Richard. *The Coherence of Theism.* Oxford: Clarendon, 1977.

Taylor, James E. *Introducing Apologetics: Cultivating Christian Commitment.* Grand Rapids: Baker Academic, 2006.

Van Til, Cornelius. *The Defense of the Faith.* 4th ed. Edited by K. Scott Oliphint. Philadelphia: Presbyterian & Reformed, 2008.

Willard, Dallas, ed. *A Place for Truth: Leading Thinkers Explore Life's Hardest Questions.* Downers Grove, Ill.: InterVarsity Press, 2010.

3. RELIGIOUS EPISTEMOLOGY, RELATIVISM AND SKEPTICISM

Allen, Diogenes. *Christian Belief in a Postmodern World: The Full Wealth of Conviction.* Louisville: Westminster John Knox, 1989.

Alston, William P. *Perceiving God: The Epistemology of Religious Experience.* Ithaca, N.Y.: Cornell University Press, 1991.

Beckwith, Francis, and Gregory Koukl. *Relativism: Feet Planted Firmly in Mid-Air.* Grand Rapids: Baker, 1998.

Boghossian, Paul. *Fear of Knowledge: Against Relativism and Con-*

structivism. Oxford: Oxford University Press, 2007.

Clouser, Roy. *Knowing with the Heart: Religious Experience and Belief in God*. Downers Grove, Ill.: InterVarsity Press, 1999.

Mavrodes, George. *Belief in God: A Study in the Epistemology of Religion*. New York: Random House, 1970.

Morris, Thomas, ed. *God and the Philosophers: The Reconciliation of Faith and Reason*. Oxford: Oxford University Press, 1994.

Moser, Paul K. *The Elusive God: Reorienting Religious Epistemology*. Cambridge: Cambridge University Press, 2008.

Newbigin, Lesslie. *Proper Confidence: Faith, Doubt and Certainty in Christian Discipleship*. Grand Rapids: Eerdmans, 1995.

Plantinga, Alvin. *God and Other Minds*. Ithaca, N.Y.: Cornell University Press, 1967.

————. *Warranted Christian Belief*. Oxford: Oxford University Press, 2000.

Swinburne, Richard. *Faith and Reason*. Oxford: Oxford University Press, 1981.

Wolterstorff, Nicholas. *Reason Within the Bounds of Religion*. 2nd ed. Grand Rapids: Eerdmans, 1984.

4. EXISTENCE OF GOD

Budziszewski, J. *Written on the Heart: The Case for Natural Law*. Downers Grove, Ill.: InterVarsity Press, 1997.

Collins, Francis S. *The Language of God: A Scientist Presents Evidence for Belief*. New York: Free Press, 2007.

Copan, Paul, and Paul K. Moser, eds. *The Rationality of Theism*. New York: Routledge, 2003.

Craig, William Lane. *The Kalām Cosmological Argument*. New York: Harper & Row, 1979. Reprint, Eugene, Ore.: Wipf & Stock, 2001.

Davies, Paul. *Cosmic Jackpot*. Boston: Houghton Mifflin, 2007.

Davis, Stephen T. *God, Reason, and Theistic Proofs*. Grand Rapids: Eerdmans, 1997.

Dembski, William A. *The Design Inference: Eliminating Chance Through Small Probabilities*. Cambridge: Cambridge University Press, 1998.

Evans, C. Stephen. *Kierkegaard's Ethic of Love: Divine Commands and Moral Obligations*. Oxford: Oxford University Press, 2004.

Gonzalez, Guillermo, and Jay W. Richards. *The Privileged Planet*. Washington, D.C.: Regnery, 2004.

Kreeft, Peter. *Heaven: The Heart's Deepest Longing*. San Francisco: Harper and Row, 1980.

Leslie, John. *Universes*. New York: Routledge, 1989.

Mascal, E. L. *He Who Is: A Study in Traditional Theism*. London: Darton, Longman, and Todd, 1966.

Mitchell, Basil. *The Justification of Religious Belief*. Oxford: Oxford University Press, 1981.

O'Connor, Timothy. *Theism and Ultimate Explanation: The Necessary Shape of Contingency*. Malden, Mass.: Blackwell, 2008.

Rea, Michael C. *World Without Design: The Ontological Consequence of Naturalism*. New York: Oxford University Press, 2002.

Ross, Hugh. *Creator and the Cosmos*. Colorado Springs: NavPress, 1995.

Strobel, Lee. *The Case for a Creator: A Journalist Investigates Scientific Evidence That Points Toward God*. Grand Rapids: Zondervan, 2004.

Swinburne, Richard. *The Existence of God*. Oxford: Clarendon, 1979.

Vitz, Paul C. *Faith of the Fatherless: The Psychology of Atheism*. Dallas: Spence, 1999.

Zacharias, Ravi. *The Real Face of Atheism*. Grand Rapids: Baker, 2004.

5. PROBLEM OF EVIL

Adams, Marilyn McCord. *Horrendous Evils and the Goodness of God*. Cornell Studies in the Philosophy of Religion. Ithaca, N.Y.:

Cornell University Press, 2000.

Beker, J. Christian. *Suffering and Hope: The Biblical Vision and the Human Predicament.* Grand Rapids: Eerdmans, 1987.

Blocher, Henri. *Evil and the Cross.* Translated by David G. Preston. Downers Grove, Ill.: InterVarsity Press, 1994.

Boyd, Gregory A. *Is God to Blame? Beyond Pat Answers to the Problem of Suffering.* Downers Grove, Ill.: InterVarsity Press, 2003.

————. *Satan and the Problem of Evil: Constructing a Trinitarian Warfare Theodicy.* Downers Grove, Ill.: InterVarsity Press, 2001.

Carson, D. A. *How Long, O Lord? Reflections on Evil and Suffering.* Grand Rapids: Baker, 1990.

Feinberg, John. *The Many Faces of Evil: Theological Systems and the Problem of Evil.* 1st ed. Grand Rapids: Zondervan, 1994.

————. *The Many Faces of Evil: Theological Systems and the Problem of Evil.* Rev. ed. Wheaton, Ill.: Crossway, 2004.

Hick, John. *Evil and the God of Love.* New York: Macmillan, 1966.

Kreeft, Peter. *Making Sense Out of Suffering.* Ann Arbor, Mich.: Servant, 1986.

Lewis, C. S. *A Grief Observed.* London: Faber & Faber, 1961.

————. *The Problem of Pain.* New York: Macmillan, 1962.

Murray, Michael. *Nature Red in Tooth and Claw: Theism and the Problem of Animal Suffering.* Oxford: Oxford University Press, 2008.

Peterson, Michael. *Evil and the Christian God.* Grand Rapids: Baker, 1982.

Plantinga, Alvin. *God, Freedom, and Evil.* New York: Harper and Row, 1974. Reprint, Grand Rapids: Eerdmans, 1977.

Reichenbach, Bruce. *Evil and a Good God.* New York: Fordham University Press, 1982.

Stackhouse, John. *Can God Be Trusted? Faith and the Challenge of Evil.* Oxford: Oxford University Press, 1998.

Swinburne, Richard. *Providence and the Problem of Evil.* Oxford:

Oxford University Press, 1998.

Van Inwagen, Peter. *The Problem of Evil.* Oxford: Oxford University Press, 2008.

Wolterstorff, Nicholas. *Lament for a Son.* Grand Rapids: Eerdmans, 1987.

Wright, N. T. *Evil and the Justice of God.* Downers Grove, Ill.: InterVarsity Press, 2006.

Yancey, Philip. *Disappointment with God: Three Questions No One Asks Aloud.* Grand Rapids: Zondervan, 1988.

6. COHERENCE OF ESSENTIAL CHRISTIAN DOCTRINES

Abraham, William J. *Crossing the Threshold of Divine Revelation.* Grand Rapids: Eerdmans, 2006.

Bauckham, Richard. *Jesus and the God of Israel.* Grand Rapids: Eerdmans, 2008.

Beckwith, Francis J. *David Hume's Argument Against Miracles: A Critical Analysis.* Lanham, Md.: University Press of America, 1989.

Bowman, Robert M., and J. Ed Komoszewski. *Putting Jesus in His Place: The Case for the Deity of Christ.* Grand Rapids: Kregel, 2007.

Brown, Colin. *Miracles and the Critical Mind.* Grand Rapids: Eerdmans, 1984.

Copan, Paul, and William Lane Craig. *Creation Out of Nothing: A Biblical, Philosophical, and Scientific Exploration.* Grand Rapids: Baker Academic, 2004.

Earman, John. *Hume's Abject Failure: The Argument Against Miracles.* Oxford: Oxford University Press, 2000.

Gathercole, Simon. *The Pre-existent Son: Recovering the Christologies of Matthew, Mark, and Luke.* Grand Rapids: Eerdmans, 2006.

Geivett, Douglas, and Gary Habermas, eds. *In Defense of Miracles.* Downers Grove, Ill.: InterVarsity Press, 1997.

Habermas, Gary R., and Michael R. Licona. *The Case for the Resur-*

rection of Jesus. Grand Rapids: Kregel, 2004.

Hurtado, Larry. *How on Earth Did Jesus Become God? Historical Questions About Earliest Devotion to Jesus.* Grand Rapids: Eerdmans, 2005.

Lewis, C. S. *Miracles: A Preliminary Study.* London & Glasgow: Collins/Fontana, 1947. Reprint, New York: HarperOne, 2001.

Licona, Michael. *The Resurrection of Jesus: A New Historiographical Approach.* Downers, Grove, Ill.: IVP Academic, 2010.

Mavrodes, George. *Revelation in Religious Belief.* Philadelphia: Temple University Press, 1988.

Ratzsch, Del. *Nature, Design, and Science: The Status of Design in Natural Science.* SUNY Series in Philosophy and Biology. Albany, N.Y.: SUNY Press, 2001.

————. *Science and Its Limits: The Natural Sciences in Christian Perspective.* 2nd ed. Downers Grove, Ill.: InterVarsity Press, 2000.

Swinburne, Richard. *The Concept of Miracle.* London; New York: Macmillan, 1971.

————. *Responsibility and Atonement.* Oxford: Oxford University Press, 1989.

————. *The Resurrection of God Incarnate.* Oxford: Oxford University Press, 2003.

————. *Revelation: From Metaphor to Analogy.* Oxford: Clarendon, 1992.

————. *Was Jesus God?* Oxford: Oxford University Press, 2008.

Walls, Jerry L. *Heaven: The Logic of Eternal Joy.* Oxford: Oxford University Press, 2002.

————. *Hell: The Logic of Eternal Damnation.* Notre Dame, Ind.: University of Notre Dame Press, 1992.

Ward, Keith. *Is Religion Dangerous?* Grand Rapids: Eerdmans, 2006.

Wierenga, Edward. *The Nature of God.* Ithaca, N.Y.: Cornell University Press, 1989.

7. BIBLICAL RELIABILITY AND THE HISTORICAL JESUS

Barnett, Paul. *Jesus and the Logic of History.* Downers Grove, Ill.: InterVarsity Press, 1997.

Bauckham, Richard. *Jesus and the Eyewitnesses: The Gospels as Eyewitness Testimony.* Grand Rapids: Eerdmans, 2006.

————. *Jesus and the God of Israel: God Crucified and Other Studies on the New Testament's Christology of Divine Identity.* Grand Rapids: Eerdmans, 2008.

Blomberg, Craig. *The Historical Reliability of John's Gospel.* Downers Grove, Ill.: InterVarsity Press, 2002.

————. *The Historical Reliability of the Gospels.* 2nd ed. Downers Grove, Ill.: InterVarsity Press, 2008.

————. *Jesus and the Gospels: An Introduction and Survey.* 2nd ed. Nashville: Broadman & Holman, 2009.

Bockmuehl, Marcus. *This Jesus: Martyr, Lord, Messiah.* Downers Grove, Ill.: InterVarsity Press, 1996.

Bruce, F. F. *The New Testament Documents: Are They Reliable?* Rev. ed. Leicester, U.K.: Inter-Varsity Press, 1960.

Copan, Paul. *Is God a Moral Monster? Making Sense of the Old Testament.* Grand Rapids: Baker, 2011.

Craig, William Lane. *The Son Rises: The Historical Evidence for the Resurrection of Jesus.* Eugene, Ore.: Wipf & Stock, 2001.

Davis, Stephen T. *Risen Indeed: Making Sense of the Resurrection.* Grand Rapids: Eerdmans, 1993.

Dunn, James D. G. *The Evidence for Jesus.* Philadephia: Westminster Press, 1986.

Eddy, Paul Rhodes, and Gregory A. Boyd. *The Jesus Legend.* Grand Rapids: Baker, 2007.

Evans, C. Stephen. *The Historical Christ and the Jesus of Faith: The Incarnational Narrative as History.* Oxford: Oxford University Press, 1996.

Evans, Craig A. *Fabricating Jesus: How Modern Scholars Distort the Gospels.* Downers Grove, Ill.: InterVarsity Press, 2006.

Habermas, Gary R. *The Historical Jesus: Ancient Evidence for the Life of Christ.* Grand Rapids: Baker, 1980.

————. *The Resurrection of Jesus: An Apologetic.* Grand Rapids: Baker, 1980.

Kitchen, K. A. *On the Reliability of the Old Testament.* Grand Rapids: Eerdmans, 2003.

Montgomery, John Warwick. *Christianity and History.* Downers Grove, Ill.: InterVarsity Press, 1964.

O'Collins, Gerald. *Jesus Risen: An Historical, Fundamental and Systematic Examination of Christ's Resurrection.* Mahwah, N.J.: Paulist, 1987.

Patzia, Arthur. *The Making of the New Testament.* Downers Grove, Ill.: InterVarsity Press, 1995.

Strobel, Lee. *The Case for Christ.* Grand Rapids: Zondervan, 1998.

Van Voorst, Robert. *Jesus Outside the New Testament: An Introduction to the Ancient Evidence.* Grand Rapids: Eerdmans, 2000.

Wilkins, Michael J., and J. P. Moreland. *Jesus Under Fire: Modern Scholarship Reinvents the Historical Jesus.* Grand Rapids: Zondervan, 1995.

Witherington, Ben. *What Have They Done with Jesus? Beyond Strange Theories and Bad History.* New York: HarperOne, 2007.

Wright, N. T. *The Challenge of Jesus: Rediscovering Who Jesus Was and Is.* Downers Grove, Ill.: InterVarsity Press, 1999.

————. *Jesus and the Victory of God.* Vol. 2 of Christian Origins and the Question of God. Minneapolis: Fortress, 1996.

————. *The New Testament and the People of God.* Vol. 1 of Christian Origins and the Question of God. Minneapolis: Fortress, 1992.

————. *The Resurrection of the Son of God.* Vol. 3 of Christian Origins and the Question of God. Minneapolis: Fortress, 2003.

8. THE CHALLENGE OF OTHER RELIGIOUS TRADITIONS

Anderson, Norman. *Christianity and the World Religions.* 2nd ed.

Downers Grove, Ill.: InterVarsity Press, 1984.

Basinger, David. *Religious Diversity: A Philosophical Assessment*. Ashgate Philosophy of Religion. Aldershot, U.K.: Ashgate, 2002.

Beckwith, Francis, and Stephen Parrish. *See the Gods Fall*. Joplin, Mo.: College Press, 2000.

Braaten, Carl. *No Other Gospel! Christianity Among the World's Religions*. Minneapolis: Fortress, 1992.

Brown, Michael L. *Answering Jewish Objections to Jesus: General and Historical Objections*. Vol 1. Grand Rapids: Baker, 2000.

————. *Answering Jewish Objections to Jesus: Theological Objections*. Vol 2. Grand Rapids: Baker, 2000.

Chapman, Colin. *Cross and Crescent: Responding to the Challenge of Islam*. Downers Grove, Ill.: InterVarsity Press, 2003.

Clark, David, and Norman Geisler. *Apologetics in the New Age*. Grand Rapids: Baker, 1990.

Corduan, Winfried. *Neighboring Faiths: A Christian Introduction to World Religions*. Downers Grove, Ill.: InterVarsity Press, 1998.

D'Costa, Gavin. *The Meeting of Religions and the Trinity*. Maryknoll, N.Y.: Orbis, 2000.

Eddy, Paul Rhodes. *John Hick's Pluralist Philosophy of World Religions*. Ashgate New Critical Thinking in Religion, Theology, and Biblical Studies. Aldershot, U.K.: Ashgate, 2002.

George, Timothy. *Is the Father of Jesus the God of Muhammad?* Grand Rapids: Zondervan, 2002.

Netland, Harold. *Dissonant Voices: Religious Pluralism and the Question of Truth*. Grand Rapids: Eerdmans, 1991.

————. *Encountering Religious Pluralism: The Challenge to Christian Faith and Mission*. Downers Grove, Ill.: InterVarsity Press, 2001.

Newbigin, Lesslie. *The Gospel in a Pluralist Society*. Grand Rapids: Eerdmans, 1989.

Ramachandra, Vinoth. *Faiths in Conflict? Christian Integrity in a Multicultural World*. Downers Grove, Ill.: InterVarsity Press,

1999.

Shorrosh, Anis. *Islam Revealed*. Rev. ed. Nashville: Thomas Nelson, 2001.

Sire, James. *The Universe Next Door*. 4th ed. Downers Grove, Ill.: InterVarsity Press, 2004.

Tennet, Timothy C. *Christianity at the Religious Roundtable: Evangelicalism in Conversation with Hinduism, Buddhism, and Islam*. Grand Rapids: Baker, 2001.

Zacharias, Ravi. *Jesus Among Other Gods*. Nashville: Thomas Nelson, 2000.

9. OBJECTIONS TO CHRISTIAN BELIEF

Barker, Dan. *Godless: How an Evangelical Preacher Became One of America's Leading Atheists*. Berkeley, Calif.: Ulysses, 2008.

Dennett, Daniel C. *Breaking the Spell: Religion as a Natural Phenomenon*. New York: Penguin, 2007.

Erhman, Bart D. *God's Problem: How the Bible Fails to Answer Our Most Important Question—Why We Suffer*. New York: HarperOne, 2008.

————. *Misquoting Jesus: The Story Behind Who Changed the Bible and Why*. New York: HarperOne, 2007.

Gale, Richard. *On the Existence and Nature of God*. Cambridge: Cambridge University Press, 1993.

Harris, Sam. *The End of Faith: Religion, Terror, and the Future of Reason*. New York: Norton, 2004.

Hitchens, Christopher. *God Is Not Great: How Religion Poisons Everything*. New York: Twelve, 2009.

Keller, James. *Problems of Evil and the Power of God*. Aldershot, U.K.: Ashgate, 2007.

Loftus, John W., ed. *The Christian Delusion: Why Faith Fails*. Amherst, N.Y.: Prometheus, 2010.

Mackie, John L. *The Miracle of Theism*. Oxford: Oxford University Press, 1983.

Martin, Michael. *Atheism: A Philosophical Justification*. Philadelphia: Temple University Press, 1992.

————, ed. *The Cambridge Companion to Atheism*. Cambridge: Cambridge University Press, 2006.

————. *The Case Against Christianity*. Philadelphia: Temple University Press, 1993.

Phillips, D. Z. *The Problem of Evil and the Problem of God*. Minneapolis: Fortress, 2005.

Price, Robert. *Deconstructing Jesus*. Amherst, N.Y.: Prometheus, 2000.

Russell, Bertrand. *Why I Am Not a Christian and Other Essays on Religion and Related Subjects*. 6th ed. New York: Simon & Schuster, 1967.

Schellenberg, J. L. *The Will to Imagine: A Justification of Skeptical Religion*. Ithaca, N.Y.: Cornell University Press, 2009.

————. *The Wisdom to Doubt: A Justification of Religious Skepticism*. Ithaca, N.Y.: Cornell University Press, 2007.

Smith, George H. *Atheism: The Case Against God*. Amherst, N.Y.: Prometheus, 1980.

Sobel, Jordan Howard. *Logic and Theism: Arguments For and Against Beliefs in God*. Cambridge: Cambridge University Press, 2009.

Spong, John Shelby. *Why Christianity Must Change or Die: A Bishop Speaks to Believers in Exile*. New York: HarperOne, 1999.

Stenger, Victor. *The New Atheism: Taking a Stand for Science and Reason*. Amherst, N.Y.: Prometheus, 2009.

NOTES

Chapter 1: What Is Christian Apologetics?

[1]Kenneth D. Boa and Robert M. Bowman Jr., *Faith Has Its Reasons: An Integrative Approach to Defending Christianity* (Colorado Springs: NavPress, 2001), p. 18.

[2]The distinction between rebutting and undercutting arguments is one I have adapted from John Pollock, who developed the distinction between rebutting and undercutting defeaters. See his *Contemporary Theories of Knowledge* (Lanham, Md.: Rowman & Littlefield, 1986), pp. 38-39.

[3]In this, I am agreeing with James Sire. He says: "The success of any apologetic argument is not whether it wins converts but whether it is faithful to Jesus." See his *A Little Primer on Humble Apologetics* (Downers Grove, Ill.: InterVarsity Press, 2006), p. 26.

[4]Rudolf Bultmann, "New Testament and Mythology," in *Kerygma and Myth*, ed. H. W. Bartsch, trans. R. H. Fuller (London: SPCK, 1953), p. 5.

[5]This point has been nicely made by John Stackhouse, *Humble Apologetics* (New York: Oxford University Press, 2002), pp. 118-19.

[6]A point nicely made by Avery Dulles: "Apologists came to recognize that every Christian harbors within himself a secret infidel. At this point, apologetics became to some extent, a dialogue between the believer and the unbeliever within the heart of the Christian himself. In speaking to his unregenerate self, the apologist assumed—quite correctly—that he would best be able to reach others similarly situated" (*A History of Christian Apologetics*, 2nd ed. [San Francisco: Ignatius, 2005], p. xx).

[7]This term was first used by John Warwick Montgomery in *Faith Founded on Fact: Essays in Evidential Apologetics* (Nashville: Nelson, 1978), p. xiii. Mark Hanna uses the neologism "metapologetics" to signify the same discipline. See his *Crucial Questions in Apologetics* (Grand Rapids: Baker, 1981), pp. 93-94.

[8]B. B. Warfield, "Apologetics," in *Studies in Theology,* The Works of Benjamin B. War-field (1932; reprint, Grand Rapids: Baker, 1981), 9:4.

[9]John Calvin, *Institutes of the Christian Religion* [1536], ed. John T. McNeill, trans. Ford Lewis Battles (Philadelphia: Westminster Press, 1960), 1.8.1, pp. 81-82.

[10]Kevin Vanhoozer, "Theology and Apologetics," in *New Dictionary of Christian Apologetics,* ed. Gavin McGrath and W. C. Campbell-Jack (Downers Grove, Ill.: InterVarsity Press, 2006), p. 35.

[11]Emil Brunner, *Dogmatik* (Zurich, 1946), 1:110.

Chapter 2: Patristic and Medieval Apologetics

[1]Avery Dulles, *A History of Christian Apologetics,* 2nd ed. (San Francisco: Ignatius, 2005), p. 1. This chapter (and, to some degree, the next) is indebted to Dulles's magisterial work.

[2]E. F. Scott, *The Apologetics of the New Testament* (New York: Putnam, 1907); F. F. Bruce, *The Defense of the Gospel in the New Testament* (Grand Rapids: Eerdmans, 1977).

[3]James Sire, *A Little Primer on Humble Apologetics* (Downers Grove, Ill.: InterVarsity Press, 2006), p. 25.

[4]Dulles, *History of Christian Apologetics,* p. 6.

[5]William Edgar, "Christian Apologetics for a New Century," in *New Dictionary of Christian Apologetics,* ed. Gavin McGrath and W. C. Campbell-Jack (Downers Grove, Ill.: InterVarsity Press, 2006), p. 4.

[6]J. K. S. Reid, *Christian Apologetics* (Grand Rapids: Eerdmans, 1969), p. 46.

[7]Dulles, *History of Christian Apologetics,* pp. 29-30.

[8]Ibid., pp. 37-38.

[9]Ibid., p. 30.

[10]Ibid., p. 32.

[11]Ibid., p. 44.

[12]Ibid., p. 73.

[13]Ibid., p. 89.

[14]Ibid., p. 84.

[15]Ibid., p. 112.

[16]Ibid., p. 91.

[17]Ibid., p. 110.

[18]Ibid., pp. 109-11.

[19]Anselm *Cur Deus homo/Why God Became Man* 1.1.

[20]Ibid., 1.2.

[21]Dulles, *History of Christian Apologetics,* p. 101.

[22]A similar argument has been made by Marilyn McCord Adams with respect to the *Proslogion.* See her "Praying the *Proslogion,*" in *The Rationality of Belief and the Plurality of Faith,* ed. Thomas Senor (Ithaca, N.Y.: Cornell University Press, 1995), pp. 13-39.

[23]Dulles, *History of Christian Apologetics,* p. 106.

24Ibid., p. 111.

25Thomas Aquinas *Summa Contra Gentiles* I:77-78; cited in Dulles, *History of Christian Apologetics*, pp. 117-18.

26Dulles, *History of Christian Apologetics*, p. 88.

27Ibid., p. 112.

28Peter the Venerable, *A Book Against the Sect or Heresy of the Saracens*; cited in Dulles, *History of Christian Apologetics*, p. 106.

29Dulles, *History of Christian Apologetics*, p. 133.

30Ibid., p. 134.

31Ibid., p. 137.

32Ibid., p. 138.

33Ibid., p. 137.

34Ibid., p. 113.

35Martin Luther, *Commentary on Galatians*, Galatians 3:6; cited in Reid, *Christian Apologetics*, p. 130.

36Luther, *Sermon on Faith and Good Works*; cited in Reid, *Christian Apologetics*, p. 131.

37Reid, *Christian Apologetics*, p. 130.

38Alister McGrath, *Intellectuals Don't Need God and Other Modern Myths: Building Bridges to Faith Through Apologetics* (Grand Rapids: Zondervan, 1993), p. 222.

39John Calvin, *Institutes of the Christian Religion*, trans. Henry Beveridge (Grand Rapids: Eerdmans, 1957), 1.4.2, p. 47.

40Calvin, *Institutes* 1.1.1, p. 37.

41McGrath, *Intellectuals Don't Need God*, p. 212.

42Calvin, *Institutes* 1.6.1, p. 64.

43Calvin, *Institutes* 1.6.2, p. 66.

44Alvin Plantinga, *Warranted Christian Belief* (New York: Oxford University Press, 2000), pp. 291-92. Plantinga is drawing upon Calvin, *Institutes* 1.7.4; 3.1.3.

45John Calvin, *Institutes of the Christian Religion* [1536], ed. John T. McNeill, trans. Ford Lewis Battles (Philadelphia: Westminster, 1960), 1.8.1, pp. 81-82.

46Dulles, *History of Christian Apologetics*, pp. 115-16.

Chapter 3: Modern and Contemporary Apologetics

1A. C. McGiffert, *Protestant Thought Before Kant* (London: Duckworth, 1911), p. 229.

2Joseph Butler, *The Analogy of Religion*, Milestones of Thought (New York: Ungar, 1961), p. 2.

3John Locke, *An Essay Concerning Human Understanding*, ed. Alexander Campbell Fraser, 2nd ed. (New York: Dover, 1959), 4.10.1, 2:306.

4Locke, *Essay Concerning Human Understanding*, 4.19.4., 2:431.

5William Lane Craig, *Reasonable Faith*, rev. ed. (Wheaton, Ill.: Crossway, 1994), p. 24.

6Blaise Pascal, *Pensées*, trans. W. F. Trotter, introduction by T. S. Eliot (New York: Dutton, 1958), n. 555, pp. 153-54.

7Craig, *Reasonable Faith*, p. 52.

[8]Pascal, *Pensées*, p. 118 n. 430.

[9]Ibid., p. 58 n. 194; see also p. 75 n. 257.

[10]Ibid., p. 74 n. 253.

[11]Ibid., p. 82 n. 289.

[12]Ibid., p. 4 n. 10.

[13]Kenneth D. Boa and Robert M. Bowman Jr., *Faith Has Its Reasons: An Integrative Approach to Defending Christianity* (Colorado Springs: NavPress, 2001), p. 37.

[14]Friedrich Schleiermacher, *On Religion*, ed. Richard Crouter, Cambridge Texts in the History of Philosophy (Cambridge: Cambridge University Press, 1996), p. 3.

[15]Karl Heinrich Sack, *Christliche Apologetik* (Hamburg, 1829; 2nd ed., 1841). See L. Russ Bush, *Classical Readings in Christian Apologetics* (Grand Rapids: Academie, 1983), p. 377; Avery Dulles, *A History of Christian Apologetics*, 2nd ed. (San Francisco: Ignatius, 2005), p. 214.

[16]Søren Kierkegaard, *Concluding Unscientific Postscript*, trans. David F. Swenson, introduction and notes by Walter Lowrie (Princeton, N.J.: Princeton University Press, 1941), p. 31.

[17]Søren Kierkegaard, *On Authority and Revelation*, trans. Walter Lowrie (Princeton, N.J.: Princeton University Press, 1955), p. 59.

[18]Søren Kierkegaard, *Concluding Unscientific Postscript to "Philosophical Fragments,"* vol. 1, *Text,* ed. Howard V. Hong and Edna H. Hong (Princeton, N.J.: Princeton University Press, 1992), p. 557.

[19]John Henry Newman, *Lectures on Certain Difficulties Felt by Anglicans in Submitting to the Catholic Church* (London, 1850; rev. ed., 1888), 2:312; cited in Dulles, *History of Christian Apologetics*, p. 247.

[20]John Henry Newman, *An Essay in Aid of a Grammar of Assent* (1870; reprint, Notre Dame, Ind.: University of Notre Dame Press, 1979), p. 300.

[21]Dulles, *History of Christian Apologetics*, pp. 247-48.

[22]Karl Barth, *Protestant Theology in the Nineteenth Century: Its Background and History,* new ed. (Grand Rapids: Eerdmans, 2002), p. 428.

[23]Karl Barth, *Church Dogmatics*, vol. 1, pt. 1, *The Doctrine of the Word of God* (Edinburgh: T & T Clark, 1936), p. 31.

[24]Humphrey Carpenter, *Tolkien: The Authorized Biography* (Boston: Houghton Mifflin, 1977), p. 151.

[25]C. S. Lewis, *God in the Dock: Essays on Theology and Ethics*, ed. Walter Hooper (Grand Rapids: Eerdmans, 1970), p. 183.

[26]*Time,* April 7, 1980, p. 66.

[27]*Letters of C. S. Lewis,* ed. W. H. Lewis (London: Bles, 1966), p. 167.

[28]C. S. Lewis, *Mere Christianity* (New York: Macmillan, 1952). *Mere Christianity* was originally given as BBC radio talks during World War II. Kenneth Boa and Robert Bowman Jr. make the startling claim that these talks "may have contributed in some measure to the Allied victory by encouraging faith and hope among the British people" (*Faith Has Its Reasons*, p. 75).

[29]Michael Maudlin, "1993 Christianity Today Book Awards," *Christianity Today* 5

(April 1993): 28; cited in Scott R. Burson and Jerry L. Walls, *C. S. Lewis and Francis Schaeffer: Lessons for a New Century from the Most Influential Apologists of Our Time* (Downers Grove, Ill.: InterVarsity Press, 1998), p. 31.

[30]C. S. Lewis, "Answers to Questions on Christianity," in *God in the Dock: Essays on Theology and Ethics,* ed. Walter Hooper (Grand Rapids: Eerdmans, 1970), p. 58.

[31]Will Vaus, *Mere Theology: A Guide to the Thought of C. S. Lewis* (Downers Grove, Ill.: InterVarsity Press, 2004), p. 21.

[32]Ibid., p. 23.

[33]Cornelius Van Til, "My Credo," in *Jerusalem and Athens: Critical Discussions on the Philosophy and Apologetics of Cornelius Van Til* (Philadelphia: Presbyterian & Reformed, 1971), p. 3.

[34]Ibid., p. 15.

[35]Cornelius Van Til, *Common Grace and the Gospel* (Philadelphia: Presbyterian & Reformed, 1972), p. 184.

[36]Cornelius Van Til, *Why I Believe in God* (Philadelphia: Committee on Christian Education of the Orthodox Presbyterian Church, n.d.), p. 20.

[37]Richard Swinburne, "Intellectual Autobiography," in *Reason and the Christian Religion: Essays in Honor of Richard Swinburne,* ed. Alan G. Padgett (Oxford: Clarendon, 1994), p. 8.

[38]Richard Swinburne, *Is There a God?* (New York: Oxford University Press, 1996), p. 2.

[39]Swinburne, "Intellectual Autobiography," p. 10.

[40]John Stackhouse, "Mind over Skepticism," *Christianity Today,* June 11, 2001, p. 1.

[41]Alvin Plantinga, "Self-Profile," in *Alvin Plantinga,* ed. James E. Tomberlin and Peter Van Inwagen, Profiles 5 (Dordrecht: Reidel, 1985), p. 33.

[42]Alvin Plantinga, "Rationality and Public Evidence," *Religious Studies* 37 (2001): 217 (italics added).

[43]Alvin Plantinga, *Warranted Christian Belief* (New York: Oxford University Press, 2000), p. 244. Cf. John Calvin, *Institutes of the Christian Religion* [1536], ed. John T. McNeill, trans. Ford Lewis Battles (Philadelphia: Westminster, 1960), 3.2.7, p. 551.

[44]Plantinga, *Warranted Christian Belief,* p. 170.

[45]See Alvin Plantinga, *God, Freedom, and Evil* (Grand Rapids: Eerdmans, 1977).

[46]Dulles, *History of Christian Apologetics,* p. xxii.

[47]Ibid.

[48]Schubert Ogden, *The Reality of God and Other Essays* (New York: Harper & Row, 1966), p. 120. See also Langdon Gilkey, "Trends in Protestant Apologetics," *Concilium* 46 (1969): 126-57.

[49]One exception is William Dyrness, *Christian Apologetics in a World Community* (Downers Grove, Ill.: InterVarsity Press, 1983).

[50]Werner Ustorf, "A Missiological Postscript," in *The Decline of Christendom in Western Europe, 1750-2000,* ed. Hugh McLeod and Werner Ustorf (Cambridge: Cambridge University Press, 2003), pp. 219-20.

[51]Harold Netland, "Introduction: Globalization and Theology Today," in *Globalizing Theology* (Grand Rapids: Baker Academic, 2006), p. 16.

Chapter 4: Varieties of Apologetics

[1]Mark Hanna, *Crucial Questions in Apologetics* (Grand Rapids: Baker, 1981), p. 94.

[2]Norman Geisler, "Apologetics, types of," in *Baker Encyclopedia of Christian Apologetics* (Grand Rapids: Baker, 1999), p. 41.

[3]Steven B. Cowan does a nice job of discussing the various ways the differences between apologetics systems can be conceptualized in "Introduction," in *Five Views on Apologetics,* ed. Steven B. Cowan (Grand Rapids: Zondervan, 2000), pp. 9-15.

[4]Bernard Ramm, *Types of Christian Apologetics* (Wheaton, Ill.: Van Kampen, 1953), pp. 7-13; *Varieties of Christian Apologetics* (Grand Rapids: Baker, 1961), pp. 14-17.

[5]For example, Cowan, "Introduction," pp. 12-14.

[6]Gordon Lewis, *Testing Christianity's Truth Claims* (Chicago: Moody Press, 1976).

[7]Cowan, "Introduction," p. 14.

[8]Geisler, "Apologetics, types of," pp. 41-44; Cowan, "Introduction," pp. 15-20.

[9]Kenneth D. Boa and Robert M. Bowman Jr., *Faith Has Its Reasons: An Integrative Approach to Defending Christianity* (Colorado Springs: NavPress, 2001), pp. 33-36.

[10]David K. Clark, *Dialogical Apologetics* (Grand Rapids: Baker, 1993).

[11]C. S. Lewis, *Surprised by Joy* (London: Fontana, 1959), p. 183.

[12]W. K. Clifford, "The Ethics of Belief," in *The Ethics of Belief and Other Essays,* ed. Timothy Madigan (Amherst, N.Y.: Prometheus, 1999), p. 77.

[13]See R. C. Sproul, John Gerstner and Arthur Lindsley, *Classical Apologetics: A Rational Defense of the Christian Faith* (Grand Rapids: Zondervan, 1984), p. 146.

[14]Here I am following the terminology of Norman Geisler, "Presuppositional Apologetics," in *Baker Encyclopedia of Christian Apologetics* (Grand Rapids: Baker, 1999), p. 607.

[15]Gordon H. Clark, *In Defense of Theology* (Milford, Mich.: Mott Media, 1984), pp. 32-33.

[16]William Alston, *Perceiving God: The Epistemology of Religious Experience* (Ithaca, N.Y.: Cornell University Press, 1991), p. 304.

[17]An argument made by Alvin Plantinga in "Rationality and Public Evidence," *Religious Studies* 37 (2001): 220-21. Plantinga makes a similar argument in *Warranted Christian Belief* (New York: Oxford University Press, 2000), p. 271 n. 56.

[18]William Lane Craig, "A Classical Apologist's Response," in *Five Views on Apologetics,* ed. Steven B. Cowan (Grand Rapids: Zondervan, 2000), p. 122.

[19]Edward Carnell, *An Introduction to Christian Apologetics* (Grand Rapids: Eerdmans, 1948), p. 169.

[20]Edward Carnell, *The Kingdom of Love and the Pride of Life* (Grand Rapids: Eerdmans, 1960), p. 6.

[21]Ibid., p. 5.

Chapter 5: Philosophical Objections to Apologetics

[1]William A. Dembski and Jay Wesley Richards, "Introduction: Reclaiming Theological Education," in *Unapologetic Apologetics: Meeting the Challenges of Theological Studies* (Downers Grove, Ill.: InterVarsity Press, 2001), p. 11.

[2]See Avery Dulles, *A History of Christian Apologetics,* 2nd ed. (San Francisco: Ignatius, 2005), pp. 326-27; Paul J. Griffiths, "An Apology for Apologetics," *Faith and Philosophy* 5, no. 4 (October 1988): 399.

[3]Richard Swinburne, *The Existence of God* (Oxford: Oxford University Press, 1979), p. 254. See also *Epistemic Justification* (Oxford: Oxford University Press, 2001), pp. 141-50; *The Existence of God,* 2nd ed. (Oxford: Oxford University Press, 2004), p. 303.

[4]Sure, one might say that the belief "my knee hurts" is publicly accessible because others can see me limping. But then the religious skeptic must explain why the belief "Jesus saves" cannot be deemed to be publicly accessible, for many people who make such a claim have had their lives transformed in very public ways.

[5]An example offered by William Alston in *A Sensible Metaphysical Realism* (Milwaukee: Marquette University Press, 2001), p. 12.

[6]Frank B. Farrell, *Subjectivity, Realism, and Postmodernism: The Recovery of the World in Recent Philosophy* (Cambridge: Cambridge University Press, 1996), p. 127; cited in Kevin Vanhoozer, "What Systematic Theology Has to Say to Analytic Philosophy (and to Postmoderns) About Postmodernity," paper presented at the Annual Meeting of the Evangelical Philosophical Society, Valley Forge, Penn., November 18, 2005, p. 3.

[7]William Dyrness, *Christian Apologetics in a World Community* (Downers Grove, Ill.: InterVarsity Press, 1983), pp. 46-50.

[8]Charles Taylor, *Sources of the Self: The Making of Modern Identity* (Cambridge, Mass.: Harvard University Press, 1989), pp. 67-68.

Chapter 6: Biblical and Theological Objections to Apologetics

[1]In Matthew 10:19 and Luke 12:11, the Greek word is *ma merimnasate;* in Mark 13:11 it is *ma promerimnate.*

[2]*Greek/English Lexicon of the New Testament and Other Early Christian Literature,* 3rd ed., rev. and ed. Frederick William Danker (Chicago: University of Chicago Press, 2000), p. 872.

[3]See the comments by Alan M. Stibbs, *The First Epistle General of Peter,* Tyndale New Testament Commentaries (Grand Rapids: Eerdmans, 1974), pp. 135-36.

[4]Albert Schweitzer, *Albert Schweitzer: Out of My Life and Thought* (New York: Mentor/ New American Library, 1953), pp. 185-86.

[5]C. Stephen Evans, "Apologetics in a New Key: Relieving Protestant Anxieties over Natural Theology," in *The Logic of Rational Theism,* ed. William Lane Craig and Mark S. McLeod (Lewiston, N.Y.: Mellen, 1990), p. 66.

[6]Austin Farrer, "The Christian Apologist," in *Light on C. S. Lewis,* ed. Jocelyn Gibb (New York: Harcourt, Brace & World, 1965), p. 26.

[7]A similar example is found in Gordon Lewis, *Testing Christianity's Truth Claims* (Chicago: Moody Press, 1976), p. 23.

[8]Ibid., p. 26.

[9]Alvin Plantinga says something similar regarding the arguments associated with natural theology in "Rationality and Public Evidence," *Religious Studies* 37 (2001):

217.

[10]J. K. S. Reid, *Christian Apologetics* (Grand Rapids: Eerdmans, 1969), p. 13.

[11]Karl Barth, *Protestant Thought: From Rousseau to Ritschl* (New York: Harper & Row, 1959), p. 323. This volume is a translation by Brian Cozens of eleven chapters of *Die Protestantische Theologie im 19. Jahrhundert* (Zurich: Evangelischer Verlag, 1952).

[12]Lewis, *Testing Christianity's Truth Claims*, p. 24.

[13]J. Gresham Machen, "Christianity and Culture," *Princeton Theological Review* 11 (1913): 7; see also his *What Is Christianity? And Other Addresses* (Grand Rapids: Eerdmans, 1951), p. 162.

[14]Dennis M. Campbell, "Why Should Anyone Believe? Apologetics and Theological Education," *Christian Century* 106, no. 4 (1989): 137.

[15]Paul J. Griffiths, *An Apology for Apologetics: A Study in the Logic of Interreligious Dialogue,* Faith Meets Faith (Maryknoll, N.Y.: Orbis, 1991), p. xii.

[16]John Stackhouse, *Humble Apologetics* (New York: Oxford University Press, 2002), p. 123.

Chapter 7: Doing Apologetics Well

[1]A number of others have utilized the map-making metaphor when describing the concept of truth. I particularly like the descriptions of John Stackhouse (*Humble Apologetics* [New York: Oxford University Press, 2002], pp. 91-95) and Kevin Vanhoozer ("Pilgrim's Digress: Christian Thinking On and About the Post/Modern Way," in *Christianity and the Postmodern Turn: Six Views,* ed. Myron B. Penner [Grand Rapids: Brazos, 2005], pp. 88-89; *The Drama of Doctrine: A Canonical Linguistic Approach to Christian Theology* [Louisville: Westminster John Knox, 2005], pp. 294-97).

[2]Nancey Murphy, "On the Nature of Theology," in *Religion and Science: History, Method, and Dialogue,* ed. W. Mark Richardson and Wesley Wildman (New York: Routledge, 1996), p. 153.

[3]William Lane Craig, *Reasonable Faith: Christian Truth and Apologetics,* rev. ed. (Wheaton, Ill.: Crossway, 1994), pp. 31-48.

[4]C. S. Lewis, *God in the Dock* (Grand Rapids: Eerdmans, 1970), p. 96.

[5]David Clark, *Dialogical Apologetics* (Grand Rapids: Baker, 1993), p. 199 (italics original).

[6]Introduction to the song "What If I Stumble?" by D.C. Talk, *Jesus Freak,* Virgin Records America, 1995.

[7]E. M. Bounds, *Power Through Prayer,* rev. ed. (Grand Rapids: Zondervan, 1962), p. 27.

[8]C. S. Lewis, "Christian Apologetics," in *God in the Dock,* ed. Walter Hooper (Grand Rapids: Eerdmans, 1970), p. 103.

Name and Subject Index

Abelard, Peter, 48
Abraham, William, 98
Adams, Marilyn McCord, 202
agnosticism, 170
Albert the Great, 51
Alston, William, 101, 206-7
Anselm, 48-49, 202
apologetic method/systems, 40,
  64, 70, 87-111
ways of categorizing, 93-96
apologetics
  academic, 26-27
  approach to, 22-23, 138,
    173-84
  audience-focused, 176-81
  audiences of, 26-29, 62
  and Christian doctrine, 18-20
  contexts of, 26, 29-31
  and culture, 85-86, 129-31
  definition, 11-34
  external, 27-28
  goals, 20-24, 92-93, 162,
    181-82
  history of, 37-82
  internal, 27-29
  limitations of, 24-26
  objections to, 56, 71, 75-76,
    84, 113-50

and persecution, 39
and personal character,
  175-76
political, 40
principles for doing well, 157-
  84
private, 26
proactive, 15-17
public, 26
and relationship to theology,
  32-34, 75
religious, 41, 46-47, 49-50,
  52-54
responsive, 15-17
and revelation, 57, 64-65, 76,
  78-79, 99
revisionist, 70, 148
and salvation, 23, 26, 104-5,
  181
in Scripture, 12-14, 37-40
success of, 22-24
traditional 70
and truth, 20-22
value and importance of,
  151-56
Aquinas, Thomas, 51-53, 88, 203
Arianism, 43, 47
Aristotle, 50-51, 56

atheism, 169-70

Augustine, 45-46, 88-89, 109

Averroes, 50-51

Bahnsen, Greg, 100

Barrett, Earl E., 94

Barth, Karl, 75-76, 82, 90, 103,
   113-14, 148-49, 204, 208

Bavinck, Herman, 75

Bellarmine, Robert, 55

Bernard of Clairvaux, 48

Blondel, Maurice, 102

Boa, Kenneth, 95, 201, 204, 206

Bounds, E. M., 182, 208

Bowman, Robert M., Jr., 201,
   204, 206

Bruce, F. F., 202

Brunner, Emil, 34, 202

Bultmann, Rudolf, 24, 201

Bush, L. Russ, 204

Buswell, J. Oliver, 94

Butler, Joseph, 63-64, 203

Calvin, John, 33, 56-58, 81,
   88-89, 110, 143, 202-3

Calvinism, 78, 98, 102

Campbell, Dennis, 154, 208

Carnell, Edward J., 94, 109, 206

Carpenter, Humphrey, 204

Christian belief
   arguments for, 9, 23, 47-48,
      51, 56-59, 62-63, 65, 67-69,
      72-74, 78-79, 81, 91-93,
      103-5, 144-45, 162-67,
      174-75

and culture, 85-86, 129-31

evidentialist objection to, 81

goal of, 167-69

and grace, 55, 104, 145-47

impediments to, 23-24,
   152-53

knowing versus showing, 167

nature of, 159-69

and proof, 162-65

and simplicity, 147-48

and sin, 57, 67, 76, 78-79, 90,
   99, 104, 141-42

and trust, 172-73

revision of, 24-25

Christianity
   globalization of, 85-86

   nature of, 17-18

Chrysostom, John, 45

Clark, David, K., 95, 206, 208

Clark, Gordon H., 94, 100, 206

classical apologetics, 95, 97, 103

Clifford, W. K., 96, 206

constructive apologetic arguments, 15, 17

contextualism
   hard, 124-25

   soft, 124

Cowan, Steven, 95, 206

Craig, William Lane, 83, 97, 167,
   203, 206, 208

cumulative case apologetics, 64,
   98

Darwin, Charles, 74

Dawkins, Richard, 170
deconstructive apologetic arguments, 15-17
deism, 62-64, 69, 71, 74
Dembski, William A., 206
Dennett, Daniel, 170
docetism, 42
Dodwell, Henry, 65-66, 89
dogma/doctrine distinction, 19-20
donatism, 45
doubt, 29
Dulles, Avery, 39, 50, 83, 201-5, 207
Dyrness, William, 205, 207
Eck, Johann, 55
eclectic apologetics, 107-11
Edgar, William, 202
Enlightenment apologetics, 61-69
Erasmus, Desiderius, 55
evangelicalism, 102-3
evangelism, 32
Evans, C. Stephen, 109-10, 207
evidentialist apologetics, 64, 95-98, 102-5, 107-11, 114, 127
    objections to, 104-5
    strict versus eclectic, 108-9
experiential apologetics, 66, 73, 96, 100-103, 105-11
    objections to, 107
    strict versus eclectic, 108-9
faith and reason, 46, 48, 51, 53-54, 68, 88-89
faithfulness to Christ, 22-24
fallibilism, 166
Farrell, Frank B., 207
Farrer, Austin, 145, 207
Feinberg, Paul, 98
fideism, 89, 95, 163, 167
Foucault, Michel, 107
Frame, John, 83, 100
Francis of Assisi, St., 175
Freud, Sigmund, 107
Galileo, 69
Geisler, Norman, 95, 97, 206
Gnosticism, 40, 42
Griffiths, Paul, 155, 208
Habermas, Gary, 98
Hackett, Stuart, 94
Hanna, Mark, 201, 206
Harris, Sam, 170
Henry, Carl F. H., 100
Herbert of Cherbury, Lord, 62-63
historical apologetics, 97-98, 103
Hitchens, Christopher, 170
Holy Spirit, role of, 23, 25, 90-91, 134-36, 145-47, 182-83
Islam, 47, 50, 52, 54, 62, 71
Judaism, 40-43, 46-47, 49-50, 52, 54, 62, 71
Justin Martyr, 43-44
Kant, Immanuel, 70
Kierkegaard, Søren, 66, 71-73, 102, 108, 110, 204

knowledge of God, 89-91,
   118-20, 125-27, 142-44
Kreeft, Peter, 83
Kuyper, Abraham, 75
late Middle Ages apologetics,
   53-54
Lewis, C. S., 76-78, 96, 102, 108,
   143, 179, 183, 204-6, 208
Lewis, Gordon, 94-95, 150,
   207-8
lifestyle apologetics, 151-52
Locke, John, 64-66, 88, 108, 203
Luther, Martin, 55-56, 58-59, 71,
   203
Machen, J. Gresham, 153, 208
Manetti, Giannozzo, 54
Manicheanism, 45-46
Manning, Brennan, 181
Marx, Karl, 107
Maudlin, Michael, 204
McDowell, Josh, 98
McGiffert, A. C., 203
McGrath, Alister, 203
medieval apologetics, 46-53, 82
Melanchthon, Philip, 56
meta-apologetic questions,
   88-93
meta-apologetics, 31
Montgomery, John Warwick, 98,
   201
Moreland, J. P., 83
Murphy, Nancey, 162, 208
natural theology, 88-89

Netland, Harold, 205
Newman, John Henry, 73-74, 88,
   204
Newton, Sir Isaac, 69
Nicholas of Cusa, 54
nineteenth-century apologetics,
   69-74
nonrealist Christianity, 170
objections to apologetics, 56, 71,
   75-76, 84, 113-50
   as-practiced versus in-princi-
      ple, 114-15
   biblical, 133-41
   the cure is worse than the
      disease, 147-49
   the irrelevance of logical
      arguments to faith, 144-45
   objection from God's tran-
      scendence, 142-44
   objection from human
      sinfulness, 141-42
   objection from postmodern-
      ism, 125-27
   objection from religious
      relativism, 120-25
   objection from religious
      skepticism, 115-20
   objection from skepticism,
      115-17
   objection from the immoral-
      ity of Christians, 127-28
   social action is more impor-
      tant, 150

sola gratia, 145-47
the white and Western
objection, 129-31
Ogden, Schubert, 83, 205
ontological argument, 49, 81
Origen, 44-45
paganism, 40-42, 44, 46-47
Pascal, Blaise, 66-69, 73, 89,
102, 110, 203
Pascal's wager, 68
patristic apologetics, 40-46, 82
Pelagianism, 45
Peter the Venerable, 49-50, 53,
203
Philo, 42
philosophy of religion, 31-32
Plantinga, Alvin, 80-81, 83, 110,
203, 205-7
Plato, 11
Pollock, John, 201
postmodernism, 84-85, 92, 103,
109, 125-27
varieties of, 125-26
practical presuppositionalism,
100
presuppositionalist apologetics,
78, 95-96, 98-100, 102-11, 114
objections to, 105-6
strict versus eclectic, 108-9
principle of credulity, 117
problem of evil, 44, 46, 81-82,
144
Ramm, Bernard, 93-95, 206

rational presuppositionalism,
100, 103
rationalism, 88, 163-64
reason, ministerial use of versus
magisterial use of, 58-59
rebutting apologetic arguments,
16-17, 201
Reformation apologetics, 55-59
Reformed apologetics, 95
Reformed theology, 88-89
Reid, J. K. S., 202-3, 208
Reimarus, Hermann Samuel, 63
relativism, 120-25
local versus global, 120-21
religious, 121-25
revelational presuppositionalism, 99-100, 103
Richards, Jay Wesley, 206
Roscelin of Compiégne, 49
Sabundus, Raimundus, 53-54,
59
Sack, Karl Heinrich, 71, 204
salvation, 23, 26
Schaeffer, Francis, 100, 108
Schleiermacher, Friedrich,
70-72, 75, 114, 148, 204
Schweitzer, Albert, 144, 207
Scott, E. F., 202
Scotus, John Duns, 53
Scripture 12-14, 37-40, 57,
64-65,
sensus divinitatis, 56-57, 110, 143
Sire, James, 38, 83, 201, 202

skepticism, 115-20, 166
  global, 115-17
  local, 115
  religious, 115-20, 207
Socrates, 11
Sproul, R. C., 97, 102, 206
Stackhouse, John, 155, 201, 205,
  208
Stibbs, Alan M., 207
Swinburne, Richard, 80, 83, 98,
  101, 108, 117, 205, 207
synergism, 89
Taylor, Charles, 130, 207
Teilhard de Chardin, Pierre, 102
theistic arguments. *See* Christian belief, arguments for
transcendental arguments, 79,
  99
truth, 21, 81, 91, 120-25, 160-63,
  167-69
    correspondence theory of, 92,
      123, 160
    and socio-linguistic context,
      123-24, 161
twentieth-century apologetics,
  74-83
twenty-first-century apologetics,
  83-86
unbelief
  affective causes of, 170
  intellectual causes of, 170-71
  nature of, 169-73
  reasons for, 25, 142
  spiritual causes of, 172
  varieties of, 169-70
undercutting apologetic arguments, 16-17, 201
Ustorf, Werner, 205
Van Til, Cornelius, 78-79, 89,
  94-95, 99-100, 105, 108, 205
Vanhoozer, Kevin, 34, 202,
  207-8
Vaus, Will, 205
Warfield, B. B., 33, 75-76, 202
William of Ockham, 53
Zeno, 42